ONLINE MARKETING STRATEGIES 2020

The Guide for Beginners to Exploit Digital Business, Work from Home and Create Passive Income with Affiliate Programs, Dropshipping, FBA, Social Media and Blogging.

George Brand

© **Copyright 2019 - All rights reserved.**

The content contained within this book may not be reproduced, duplicated or transmitted without direct written permission from the author or the publisher.

Under no circumstances will any blame or legal responsibility be held against the publisher, or author, for any damages, reparation, or monetary loss due to the information contained within this book. Either directly or indirectly.

Legal Notice:

This book is copyright protected. This book is only for personal use. You cannot amend, distribute, sell, use, quote or paraphrase any part, or the content within this book, without the consent of the author or publisher.

Disclaimer Notice:

Please note the information contained within this document is for educational and entertainment purposes only. All effort has been executed to present accurate, up to date, and reliable, complete information. No warranties of any kind are declared or implied. Readers acknowledge that the author is not engaging in the rendering of legal, financial, medical or professional advice. The content within this book has been derived from various sources. Please consult a licensed professional before attempting any techniques outlined in this book.

By reading this document, the reader agrees that under no circumstances is the author responsible for any losses, direct or indirect, which are incurred as a result of the use of the information contained within this document, including, but not limited to errors, omissions, or inaccuracies.

Table of Contents

Introduction 9

Chapter 1: Online Marketing — What Is It? 13

What Is Marketing? 13

How Does Online Marketing Work? 16

Different Marketing Strategies for Different Businesses 20

Chapter Summary 23

Chapter 2: The Most Important Tools 25

Tools That You Need for Online Marketing 25

The Power of Your Opt-In Page 27

Working with Autoresponders 30

Leveraging a Sales Funnel 37

Chapter Summary 39

Chapter 3: Method – What to Do and What Not to Do 41

Do Not Obsess Over Other Marketers 42

Do Not Sell Low Ticket Items 44

Do Not Stand Still to Seek Accuracy 46

Do Leverage Video Content 47

Do Create a Strong Facebook Presence 51

Do Start Your Own Blog 53

Do Take Advantage of Email Marketing 55

Learn How to Produce High-Quality Copy 56

Chapter Summary 58

Chapter 4: Positioning 60

What Positioning Is and Why You Need It 61

Positioning Is Not a Guarantee 63

Positioning Through Your Brand Identity 64

Positioning Through Your Products and Services 66

Positioning Through Your Price Points 68

Positioning Through Your Location 70

Positioning Through Your Marketing Strategy 71

Receiving Feedback About Your Position 73

Managing Your Position in the Market 74

Chapter Summary 76

Chapter 5: No Traffic, No Money 78

How Paid Online Marketing Strategies Work 79

Leveraging Facebook Ads to Land Leads 82

Other Social Media Paid Advertising Strategies 87

The Power of Google Paid Advertisements 89

Chapter Summary 94

Chapter 6: A License to Make Money – Your List 96

What an Email List Affords You 97

How to Use Your Email List in Marketing 99

Growing Your Email List in 3 Easy Steps 100

   Step One: Create 6-12 Opt-In Freebies............. 101

   Step Two: Promote Your Freebies 103

   Step Three: Send Out Regular E-Newsletters..... 105

Chapter Summary 106

Chapter 7: Online Marketing Is a Business 108

You Need the Right Approach 109

You Must Start with a Budget 112

You Are Nothing Without a Profitable Market 115

You Need to Be Passionate About What You Do..... 117

You Must Improve Your Competency 120

Chapter Summary 122

Chapter 8: The Winning Mindset 125

Learn How to Motivate Yourself 127

Always Look for the Solution 130

Consistency Is Key in Your Success 132

Hone in on Your Courage to Jump 134

Overcome Your Fear of Failure............................. 136

Cultivate a Sense of Resiliency 139

Have Someone You Can Look Up To 140

Chapter Summary 142

Chapter 9: It's Your Time 144

Conclusion 152

Introduction

Online marketing is one of the most relevant and powerful skills that you can have in today's world. When it comes to online marketing, there are countless reasons that you should get involved as soon as possible. The first and possibly most obvious reason that you should get involved with online marketing is that online marketing provides you with an excellent skill set to earn money from the internet, which is an incredible opportunity in today's world. Not only will working from the internet provide you with a wonderful income opportunity, but it can also provide you with a great passive income opportunity and the power of time freedom, which is quite possibly more valuable than financial freedom.

Another huge benefit of getting into online marketing is that it costs next to nothing to get started with. Many people start with less than $200 and find themselves consistently earning upward of $1,000, $10,000, and even $100,000 every single month within just a few months of starting their online marketing businesses. If you want to get involved in the form of a career that earns you massive cash, that has no cap to what you can earn, and that puts you directly in control over your workload, online marketing is an excellent opportunity for you.

You might have come under the impression that online marketing is only plausible for the lucky few who have made it work, but the truth is: it is a tried-and-true method that works time and again for anyone willing to truly invest in learning how. Something tells me that you already suspect this to be true, too, which is exactly why you are here right now learning about how you can get involved with online marketing.

As e-commerce and online marketing continue to mature, it is no secret that the market is definitely more saturated than it was just five to ten years ago. That being said: many people are getting involved and are not educating themselves on the best possible skills to succeed. As a result, they are not creating the level of success that they could create for themselves, which leaves plenty of room for other people (*that's you!*) to come in and take over.

If you are ready to step up into the new age of business and start earning money from your computer, regardless of where you are situated in the world, it is time for you to start educating yourself on online marketing. This means that you need to learn about the tested methods *that actually work*, and not just the strategies that have been repeated over and over in the most generic way possible on nearly every blog out there.

Yes, I said it: not every piece of knowledge you can get your hands on offers you the high quality, a powerful skill set that will set you apart from your competition and get you ahead in the business.

You *must* learn how to qualify the information that you receive and validate whether or not it is worth applying in your business to ensure that the strategies you are using will work toward your success. In the world of e-commerce and online marketing, if it takes you too long to start generating momentum, chances are you will give up before you ever generate any success. The key is to come in hot and heavy, sweep through the market, and generate a massive buzz around your business while rapidly building on the momentum that you are gaining as you go. The more you can master the art of momentum and proper online marketing strategies, the greater your success will be in online marketing.

If you are ready to take a dive into this powerful income earning the opportunity and changing your life and income with online marketing, then it is time for you to get started! Please make sure that as you read through this book, you are constantly considering how you can apply this knowledge to your real-life situation in a way that serves your momentum and success. With this outlook, you will be sure to have great success in your online marketing business!

Chapter 1: Online Marketing — What Is It?

"Marketing is telling the world you're a rock star. Content marketing is showing the world you are one."
— Robert Rose

What Is Marketing?

In the most basic sense of the word, marketing is promoting products or services, conducting market research, and advertising. When we think of marketing, we often think of businesses exclusively, but the reality is that we actually engage in marketing behaviors regularly. In our personal lives, we often promote things we like or are interested in so that other people will partake with us, or will begin to use those products or services in their own lives. For example, let's say you want to watch a movie with your friends. If you talk about how great your favorite movie is and how much they will love it, you are promoting your favorite movie. If the promotion is successful, they will choose to watch your favorite movie, and you are rewarded with the benefit of getting to watch the movie.

When you choose to take on a marketing role, such as with online marketing, your entire purpose is to get people interested in your company's product or service so that they will buy it. In business, marketing often comes with the sole purpose of earning a financial profit, as you desire to sell your company's goods in exchange for money. Marketing takes place in product development, distribution methods, sales, and advertising, as all of these areas of the business contribute to your ability to promote the product. If you engage in marketing in every possible way, you can feel confident that you will be able to successfully encourage people to invest in your products.

Marketing as we know it began in the 1950s when the television and radio and, later, the internet all became ways for people to communicate with each other. Businesses took advantage of these communication methods and began to promote their products and services on them, effectively reaching the ears and eyes of everyone who had these products or services present in their households. As a result, they could increase their profits because they were making a bigger impact in reaching people and spreading awareness about the products or services they had available. They were also able to generate better relationships with their customers because it felt like they were in their homes with them, which was previously a space that was only open to friends and family that the household knew. This inclusion of the advertising companies in their homes created a sense of intimacy or closeness in the relationships that people began sharing with companies, which further improved customer loyalty and willingness to purchase from the said company.

How Does Online Marketing Work?

When it comes to online marketing, the approach that businesses use is quite different from other marketing strategies. When it comes to marketing in the physical world, your resources are somewhat limited to print, radio, television, and word of mouth. When it comes to marketing in the digital world, however, you tap into a wide variety of resources that you can use to help you get your products and services in front of the eyes of customers. In a sense, online marketing is somewhat like digging into a completely new virtual world and sharing your products or services in a totally new way. For that reason, it does take some effort and education to understand what online marketing is and the various ways that you can approach it in order to get in touch with your audience and make sales.

When it comes to leveraging web-based sales channels for online marketing, there are several different channels that you can use to earn sales from. Online marketing is often done through paid advertisements, search engine optimization (SEO), email marketing, social media marketing, and blogging. Most online marketers will pick one or two marketing channels to leverage and will commit to mastering those channels before adding others. This way, they can guarantee the results of the said channel before moving on to the next channel that they were interested in using.

By the time an online marketing company has matured, they will likely be using all of the aforementioned sales channels to generate sales from. This is because online marketing makes each channel incredibly accessible, so it does not make sense *not* to tap into every single channel and generate results from it. So long as it is done in a sustainable manner that establishes actual results, leveraging each channel can be a powerful way to maximize your income and generate the largest momentum through online marketing.

In addition to what channels exist, it is also a good idea to understand how each channel is leveraged to actually generate a marketing effort that results in sales and profits for the business. The way that different channels are turned into marketing channels is rather simple. In fact, it happens over just six steps, starting with researching the market and ending with earning profits.

The first step, researching the market, is often done even before a product is chosen to market to the public. For successful businesses, market research is done first to help the company find out which industry and niche will offer the most profits for their business. If a company is already established, they will still do research to identify which of their existing products performs best through a certain channel so that they can market something likely to make sales through that particular channel. If they cannot find a product that they sell that will serve that particular channel, many companies will introduce a new product to sell to earn money through that channel.

Next, the company will choose what they are going to sell. This is a simple step that often comes through as the logical answer to the results of the research that they have already conducted. When the company chooses what they are going to sell, it always clearly fits into their niche and brand to maintain the same image across every channel that they are using online and offline.

The third step involves the company taking the time to create a marketing strategy for that channel. Each channel will either have its own sales funnel or fit into a greater sales funnel that leads people to the checkout page to purchase products or services from the company. The strategy is always well-researched based on what is most likely to work for that channel, and then it is written down so that it can clearly be followed like a set of guidelines for that particular platform as they go forward.

After they have created their strategy, companies will devote time to executing the strategy. Companies will often have an allotted period of time that they will commit to executing the original strategy before they begin to analyze the results of their strategy so that they can adapt and evolve the strategy to produce better results. Typically, this window starts around one week and moves out toward one month. Once that particular channel matures, and the company has successfully been earning profits from it, they will typically only check the analytics once every other month or every three months to ensure that it is still producing positive results. Otherwise, they let it continue to run based on their current marketing plan so that it can produce analytics for their company that they can use to create marketing strategies for the future of their company.

After that allotted window of time has gone by, the fifth step is for companies to begin looking into their accumulated analytics. They look at who was purchasing, how well their strategies were performing, and what particular behaviors or elements of the strategy were contributing to those sales. They also look at what part of the strategy was not working so that they can begin to understand where that particular part of the marketing strategy fell flat. Through understanding what their customers want more of, and what they want less of, marketers are able to adapt and evolve their strategies to continue to create a more desirable customer experience. As a result, they increase their profitability by earning more sales through their chosen sales channel.

The final step in the entire strategy is earning profits. Profits are more of a result of a reward for an effective strategy and an effective execution of the strategy, rather than an actual strategy. That being said, they are leveraged into the strategy as marketers will use the proportion of profits as a part of their analytics to gauge whether or not their strategies are actually working. If they are not, it will show as the profits will be minimal, stale, or declining rather than steadily building momentum and increasing over time.

Different Marketing Strategies for Different Businesses

Each online marketing business is going to require its own unique marketing strategy to ensure that you are getting your product or service in front of the eyes of your target audience. When it comes to different marketing strategies, you will notice that each brand does a slightly different take on standard marketing strategies to ensure that they serve their unique client in the best way possible. These differences are designed to ensure that the business is able to leverage its chosen business model while still reaching and effectively selling to its target audience. Since each audience has their own unique preferences and needs, this is necessary in order to gain their interest and earn their business.

When it comes to online marketing, there are three big strategies that tend to serve as guidelines for the way that marketing will be done. One of these includes private online marketing, which includes you running your own private business with your own products or services. This particular structure allows you to market in virtually any way that you desire because you are the one entirely in charge of what it is that you are doing. You can use social media sales funnels, paid advertisements, and other forms of organic and paid marketing strategies to get your audience to your website. Truly, the sky is the limit. That being said, if you do choose to run everything by yourself, you are going to have a lot of moving parts to manage on your own. In addition to being responsible for marketing, you are also going to be responsible for stocking products or fulfilling services, and managing all of the elements of your business that go into maintaining an online store. For example, you will have to manage your website and all of the working parts of your website, such as shopping carts, product pages, and check out links.

An alternative to doing everything yourself is to choose to sell on a platform such as Amazon. Amazon selling is a business model that allows you to completely reduce your involvement with the business side of things so that all you have to do is worry about marketing and products. If you choose to use a service such as Amazon FBA, you can even minimize your involvement with products to the point where all you need to do is purchase them and have them shipped to Amazon to be taken care of. Creating a marketing strategy with Amazon is often as simple as identifying your target audience, finding the right products to serve them, and then marketing through paid advertisements and social media to get as much traffic to your website as possible. If you really want to minimize and simplify your strategy, you can even cut out organic marketing and rely solely on paid advertisements, such as those that can be hosted directly through Amazon's Ad Manager Service.

The third form of an online business model that you could use to leverage online marketing with is known as "influencing" and requires you to solely focus on online marketing. When it comes to influencing, you are not required to host a business or deal with products in any way, whatsoever. Instead, you market yourself as a personality and then market other people's products and businesses to your audience as they begin to grow and trust you. This way, you solely specialize in marketing, and you are not required to do anything else business-related online. Influencing is still a fairly involved business; however, as you will need to put in the effort to specialize in marketing and grow your audience into one that trusts in you.

Chapter Summary

Online marketing is the go-to method for making money online. Online marketing accounts for virtually every form of business that uses the internet to promote their products or services to their audience, which means that if you want to earn an income from the internet, you need to know how to leverage online marketing.

Creating an online marketing strategy should be made as simple as possible early on to not confuse yourself or make things more complex than they need to be. When it comes to marketing online, you should be seeking to create results with each strategy that you use before adding a new element to the strategy. Ideally, your earliest strategy should have no more than three or four steps to get your customers from identifying who you are to purchasing your products. This way, there is less for you to manage which means that you will have an easier time getting a feel for how online marketing works, how to read your analytics, and how to evolve your strategy to produce better results every time.

Chapter 2: The Most Important Tools

"The best marketing doesn't feel like marketing."
— Tom Fishburne

Tools That You Need for Online Marketing

Creating your online marketing strategy might seem challenging if you are not familiar with the tools that people use to actually leverage online marketing. If you are brand new to the industry, you might not realize that there are tools like autoresponders, opt-in pages, and various other tools that can be used to market your business. These tools are not only essential, but they are also able to be automated so that you do not have to manually attempt to grow your business online. In fact, automation is the biggest benefit of online marketing: you can create a sales funnel that continues to earn you income over a period of time, without you ever having to manually do anything beyond managing the funnel to keep it continue working.

When it comes to getting started with your online marketing business, there are three tools that you absolutely must leverage in order to succeed, regardless of whether you are running your own business or leveraging Amazon or affiliate marketing. Those include the aforementioned autoresponders and opt-in pages, as well as sales funnels. Without these three tools in place, you will have a hard time getting your business in front of your audience and converting brand recognition into sales so that you can become profitable. Fortunately, these tools are easy to understand and even easier to fix into place for you to begin earning an income in your business. In this chapter, we will explore what these three tools are, how they work, and how you can leverage them to grow your online marketing business.

The Power of Your Opt-In Page

The first tool that you need to have when it comes to launching an online business is an opt-in page. When it comes to online marketing, *nothing* is guaranteed except for your email list, so it is mandatory that you begin to capture emails from day one. If you are not capturing emails, you could find yourself struggling to stay in touch with your audience in the most effective way possible. Social media platforms can have failures and have had them from time to time in the past couple of years, where one or multiple parts of the platform was not working. If you cannot get in touch with your customers, you cannot market to them, which means that they cannot buy from you. For an online marketer, this could be detrimental to your sales numbers.

Creating an email list means that even when the social media platforms, or any other platforms such as your website, are down, you can still get in touch with your audience. This way, you can keep them in the loop and help them continue to do business with you no matter what goes on.

Your email list is not just about other platforms going down, either. Although this is the most important and reliable form of contact that you have with your audience, it also happens to be one of the easiest for you to create and automate so that you can generate sales without any manual marketing efforts. In other words, you can completely automate an entire sales funnel through an opt-in page and email autoresponders so that you are earning money without ever having to actually do anything to make it happen. Other than, of course, getting people to land on your opt-in page in the first place.

Your opt-in page can be made in one of two ways. The first way involves you using a built-in opt-in page creator on your website if you already have one. Platforms like Squarespace and WordPress have features where you can create an opt-in page or opt-in popup right there on your hosting platform so that you can begin to generate your list. The second way is to use a third-party platform that offers the opportunity for you to create opt-in pages so that you can capture emails. Third-party pages are excellent if your host does not offer this service, although you do want to make sure that the two can be integrated to ensure that you can actually lead people to this page effortlessly. They are also excellent if you are not using your own website at all, as you can create a simple landing page with your own domain and generate leads that way.

If you are going to use a third-party opt-in page creator, consider using a third party that also offers autoresponder and e-newsletter features so that you can do everything from one convenient place. Get Response, Constant Contact, and MailChimp are all great platforms to check out if you need a platform that provides all of these features in one easy location.

When you build your platform, your goal is to make it as simple as possible. You want everything on the page to draw peoples' attention to the part where they input their information and get signed up on their list. If you have anything drawing them elsewhere, they could get distracted, and then you could miss out on a possible capture. Ideally, the page should be simple with a plain background, an image of you or another person who provides a friendly feel, and then the part where they can add their email. You should also include some basic information on what they can expect from signing up for your e-newsletter, such as what incentive you are offering and what types of emails they will receive.

Offering incentives is commonplace for email opt-ins these days, as they give people a reason to offer you their email. Opt-in incentives often include things like a free digital product download, a discount, an exclusive product or service, or something else that they can only receive from signing up for your email. Ideally, this item should be free or low-cost for you to make and supply and should be interesting enough that your customers actually want to sign up to receive it. That way, they feel compelled to do so, and you are not giving away too much, resulting in you cutting into your bottom line.

After you have designed a simple opt-in page, you need to make sure that it is properly configured to work with your autoresponder. This ensures that when people sign up, they actually receive the automated emails that offer the incentive, as well as other important information about your brand and how they can do business with you. You will learn more about autoresponders below.

Working with Autoresponders

Autoresponders are a form of communication technology that allows businesses to create automated communications with their customers, rather than always having to respond manually. Although autoresponders are not intended to completely replace communications in your business, they are a powerful tool that can help you boost your productivity and earn more sales.

The most popular form of autoresponders and the one that has been the longest standing is email autoresponders. Email autoresponders are e-newsletters that automatically get sent out to your email list, or certain parts of it, based on parameters you set into place. For example, if you sign up for a new email newsletter from your favorite blogger and immediately receive a "welcome" email, you have received an email from an autoresponder. In addition to the traditional email autoresponders, this particular technology has now also been plugged into certain social media platforms. These autoresponders can be used to provide automated messages to your customers any time they message your business page. This way, whenever someone messages you, they immediately receive a message that thanks them for getting in touch with you and that provides them with additional information that may be relevant. For example, you might provide them with an idea of when they can expect a message back by or a brief message informing them of ways to get in touch with you for specific inquiries that you may not manage on social media, such as service concerns. These autoresponders are helpful as they support you with maintaining a stronger "response rate" on your page, which is a rating that you receive for responding quickly to the people that are messaging you.

When it comes to generating sales online, autoresponders will be a part of the third step in getting people to buy from you. As you already know, the first step is being discovered, and the second step is having your follower opt-in so that they can agree to receive more marketing materials from you through methods such as email. This means that you want to have your autoresponder set up in a way that gives thanks to the individual for choosing to get in touch with you or stay in communications with you after discovering your business. This way, you are expressing gratitude for their interest, and you are increasing your chances of building a positive and strong relationship with that individual.

Autoresponders are a crucial part of your sales funnel because they provide you with the opportunity to quickly and efficiently stay in touch with your audience. This way, you do not have to attempt to manually run an online business because, instead, you can let it be run automatically. Automation not only takes some of the pressure off of yourself, but it also helps you create more consistency and accuracy in your business. This way, rather than people waiting anywhere from a few hours to several days to receive a welcome email and information on how they can follow you elsewhere online, they receive that information immediately and at any of your scheduled times. You can also use these forms of automation to generate automated newsletters with updates about your business so that rather than having to send out emails on specified days, you can spend a single day writing and scheduling them. As a result, they are guaranteed to go out on time, and they have all of the most relevant information for that time period in your business. When it comes to running an online business, this makes it significantly easier and more effective than nearly any other tool out there.

There are many different autoresponders that you can use to help you run your business, but the best ones are already built into email marketing platforms that you can use in your business. This way, rather than adding unnecessary accounts and steps into the process, you can easily set everything up and operate from one familiar and simple platform. The best platforms for this include MailChimp, Constant Contact, GetResponse, and Benchmark. Each of these is simple to use and has affordable options for getting started with so that you are not spending unnecessary amounts on this part of your business early on. Ideally, you want to pick a platform that is going to offer you everything that you need right now and as you continue to grow your business so that you do not have to attempt to port your contacts over to a new platform should you decide to change once you grow. That said, invest in the best platform that you can afford for your business at this time, and choose the tier that is most relevant to where you are already at in business so that you are not spending any more than you need to at this time. You can always upgrade your package later as your list begins to outgrow the basic package.

After you have chosen what platform you want to use, you will need to decide how your autoresponder is going to work into your strategy. The most basic way to set up an autoresponder and incorporate it into your strategy is to have your responder send out three automated emails once someone signs up to receive your newsletter. The first email will be a thank you email, the second will include some discount codes, and the third will include your social media handles for people to follow you online. Each email needs to be designed properly in order to capture your new lead's attention so that you can ensure that the email is opened and that the lead takes action.

Your first email, or your welcome email, should be basic. People are often turned off by lengthy or overwhelming welcome emails, so you want to make sure that you have one that is simple and straightforward. You have to start this email by saying thank you, which helps to boost your charisma, give a personal feel to the email, and build your relationship with your customer. If you have promised some form of incentive to subscribe, you want to make sure that this is included in your very first email. *Do not* write more than one email to go out on the first day, as this comes across as *spammy* and will lead people to believe that you will always bombard them with too many emails. It can rapidly lead to people unsubscribing right away to avoid getting too many emails from you. The last part of your "thank you" email should be expectations around when the subscriber can expect to receive new emails. For example, if you offer a weekly, bi-weekly, or monthly newsletter that is filled with the latest information on your business, set that expectation so that the subscriber knows when to receive emails from you, and what might be stored inside of them. You can also ask your subscribers to "whitelist" you, or mark you as an approved sender, so that your emails go to their inbox and not their spam box where they would get overlooked and, as a result, cost you in sales down the line.

Your second email should include another incentive for them to open the email, such as an exclusive coupon code or a discount on certain products that they gain access to for being a new subscriber. This email should go out exactly one week later and should be used to serve as a reminder for your subscriber to take a look at your products or services that you have available for sale. Many times, subscribers will open your welcome email and will take a look at what offers you have and consider buying from you, but then decide to buy later. If you do not follow up, they might forget about you and buy from someone else who took the time to follow up and remind them about their offers. This email, again, should be fairly simple and should feature a coupon code or a discount that incentivizes them to open the email and shop with your business.

The final autoresponder email that you need to have to set up your autoresponder for your sales funnel should be sent two to three weeks later and should invite people to follow you on social media. This email gives you the opportunity to expand your reach so that you can market to them in more ways than one, and in the way that *they* chose to be marketed to. This way, they are more likely to pay attention to you and continue to follow your business so that eventually they buy from you, or they become repeat buyers.

Once you have all three of these autoresponders in place, you have the most basic set up for a sales funnel running through your email system. With this organized, you actually have no reason to touch your email other than to send out newsletters should you choose to use e-newsletters as an opportunity to keep your customers up to date with your latest offers and sales.

Leveraging a Sales Funnel

In the previous two sections, we outlined a basic sales funnel that consists of an opt-in page and an autoresponder that sends out emails to encourage people to buy from you. Since you want to keep things simple, this is a completed sales funnel that can earn sales time and again so long as you continue to drive traffic to your opt-in page. With that being said, you will need to conceptualize one more element of your sales funnel so that you can turn this into a successful funnel that earns you an incredible income. That is: you need to conceptualize where the traffic is coming from.

The easiest way to drive traffic into your sales funnel is through social media. Most brands and businesses will generate a presence on social media and will feature links and captions that encourage people to go to their website. There, they find the landing page or the opt-in pop up that allows for them to sign up for e-newsletters and receive the incentives, while also getting them on your contact list. Ideally, you should use social media as your initial method for getting traffic onto your opt-in page so that you can grow your list.

Other ways that you can reach your customers include paid advertisements, blogging, affiliates, and word of mouth marketing. The more you can tap into these methods and drive people to your links, the more success you will have. That being said, you have to make sure that you are taking proper measures to share your links and encourage people to join your list in a way that does not come across as spammy or pushy. People are not going to want to visit your links or sign up with you if you are creating posts that sound like the only thing that you care about is getting people on your list so that you can sell to them. Instead, they want to build a relationship with you and feel as though they are a part of your community, and that being a part of your email list brings them even closer into your community. This way, they feel a sense of trust in you, and they are more likely to actually pay attention to what you are saying and what you are asking of them when you do ask for sales. We will talk more about how you can market your business without sounding spammy in Chapter 7.

Chapter Summary

When it comes to growing your online marketing business, you need to have three specific tools in place to help you get started. These tools contribute to you having a sales funnel, which helps guide people toward the checkout button on your sales pages. Creating a strong sales funnel comes from having a simple opt-in page with a strong incentive and autoresponders that immediately offer people the incentive and routinely remind them that your business exists.

By having these tools properly fixed in place for your sales funnel, you can feel confident that your business is going to consistently generate sales for your business. The best part is, this entire basic funnel is automated, meaning that you do not have to take the time to manually process any part of it. Once it is fixed in place, you simply need to drive traffic into the funnel to encourage sales to take place in your business.

It is extremely important that you do not overlook sales funnels in your business and the tools that help you grow your sales funnels, as these are essential for growing momentum in your business. There has been speculation in the past that sales funnels are tacky or outdated, but this is largely due to the fact that people in the early-to-mid 2010s were building and promoting them in a way that came across as spammy. As a result, people have grown frustrated with and tired of the older way of building sales funnels, which often included "educational videos" and several hoops that people had to jump through in order to officially buy the product. By creating one that is simple, straightforward, and transparent, you increase your chances of getting people onto your list and making sales in a way that stays in integrity with a strong and honest brand.

Chapter 3: Method – What to Do and What Not to Do

"Our jobs as marketers are to understand how the customer wants to buy and help them to do so."
— *Bryan Eisenberg*

One of the best parts of online marketing, now, being a mature industry, is that we have clearly identified what you should do and what you should not do when it comes to this particular marketing opportunity. Knowing the guidelines as to what is expected or ideal and what is not expected or not ideal for growing your business and making an income from your chosen opportunity is important.

In this chapter, we will discuss three things that you should absolutely not do in your business and five things that you should do to kick start your growth. Understand that this advice comes from the hands-on experiences of countless entrepreneurs who have come before you and paved the way for you to generate success in your online marketing business. While you can certainly ignore these if you desire, I suggest you don't. Following these simple steps is the easiest guide to help propel you toward success much faster in your online marketing business.

Do Not Obsess Over Other Marketers

One of the biggest mistakes that new marketers make when they launch their online businesses includes obsessing over other marketers. A piece of advice frequently given to new marketers is to take a look at the competition to identify what the latest trends are, as well as to be inspired for how you might consider marketing your own business. This is and always will be true, but many new marketers do not know how to use this as a tool without turning it into a game of comparison. When it comes to looking to other marketers for inspiration and ideas, it is important that you do not obsess over what they are doing.

Excessively fixating on what other marketers are doing and how they are growing their businesses is an excellent way for you to tank your own business for many reasons. First, many people who engage in this behavior find themselves feeling inadequate, or like they lack the necessary skills and talents to generate a successful business online. This intense self-doubt can lead to you struggling to actually grow your business, which can result in you experiencing major setbacks to your success. You might also find that the more you obsess over other people's marketing strategies, the less you give yourself creative freedom. Instead of being inspired and creating your own unique brand, you might find yourself trying to copy another brand out there, which can lead to you stunting the growth of your own business by cutting off your unique edge. Another big mistake that commonly happens when this behavior takes place is that marketers find themselves switching strategies too quickly as they attempt to "keep up" with everyone else. By rapidly switching strategies, they end up confusing and ultimately losing their audience due to not being able to provide a clear and consistent brand experience.

If you want to really expand your business in online marketing, you need to give yourself time to slow down and build your own brand. Do not be afraid to look at other marketers for inspiration or advice, but refrain from getting caught up in any obsessions over how people are growing their businesses. It can feel scary to believe in your own ability to make something equally as successful, if not more successful, than your competition, but trust that it is possible and that with consistent and intentional efforts, you will succeed in doing so.

Do Not Sell Low Ticket Items

A big rut that many online marketers fall into involves selling low ticket items. When it comes to generating success online, low ticket items are never the way to go because low ticket items require high volume sales for you to generate enough income to make it worth it. Once you factor in the cost of running your business, such as your Amazon account expenses or your website fees, plus advertising costs, there is not enough of a profit to make it worth it. Even if you have the funds to pay for the enormous amounts of advertising that you would need to drive enough traffic to your page to reach these volumes of sales, you do not yet have a reputation strong enough to make that volume matter. People who landed on your page would still not have a clue as to who you were, and it would take time for you to build up a reputation strong enough to create a sustainable business. In the end, it will feel like you are pushing a bike up the hill while its brake is engaged. It's possible, but it's incredibly challenging and virtually pointless.

Instead of selling low ticket items, switch out for medium to high ticket items that are going to earn you larger profit margins. Most marketers say do not settle for anything that generates less than a 30% profit margin, as you will not have enough of a margin to reasonably manage sales or earn a decent income from your business. As you look for products or services to sell, make sure that you have a 30% profit margin *after* you factor in the cost of the item or service *plus* the cost of running your business. You need to make sure that you can afford to keep your systems in place while also earning a strong profit off of your business, as this will make it worthwhile.

When you switch to selling medium to high ticket items, the larger profit margins mean that you do not need as high of sales volumes. This means that you will not require as large of a marketing budget and that you afford yourself time to build your reputation so that you can increase your momentum and further grow your business. Over time, you can add a few low ticket "entry-level" items to encourage people to buy from your business and get a feel for who you are and what you offer. Or you might consider adding low ticket add-on items that people buy after they have purchased a high-ticket item. Otherwise, everything else should be a medium-to-high ticket to ensure that you have generated enough of an income in your business to make it profitable and worth your efforts.

Do Not Stand Still to Seek Accuracy

When it comes to marketing, good enough is good enough. Even larger companies and massive corporations make mistakes in their marketing campaigns or their systems, and people still are loyal to these businesses and shop with them regularly. That is not just because they are already well-known and loved by their customers, but also because customers are not actually as nit-picky as we believe they will be when we first start out in our business.

Getting caught up with perfectionism is only going to lead to you struggling to go public with your business because you will be fighting to make every little thing perfect. You will read, re-read, re-write, and re-read your content and marketing materials over and over again, constantly tweaking them and refining them in an effort to achieve a level of perfection that even you are not totally sure of what it is.

Instead of holding yourself up to impossible standards that even the best marketers out there do not hold themselves against, start to become comfortable with doing your best and leaving room for growth. Even if you do notice an error, later on, you can always tweak it or use it as a lesson to help you do better in the future when you run similar marketing campaigns. There is nothing wrong with making a mistake or leaving room for growth, as this is all a part of the business. Be patient with the process and trust that good enough is, in fact, good enough for you to make money from.

Do Leverage Video Content

Video content has grown exponentially in the past five years, to the point where it is now the most popular form of marketing on the internet. If you want to grow your business quickly, you will need to be willing to leverage video content so that you can get in front of your audience in a way that they are readily willing to receive. The biggest reason why video content has grown so popular is that it adds back the personal touch that the internet tends to lack otherwise. With video, you can show people who you are, generate a face-to-face relationship with them, and even do product demos and help physically show them what you are talking about in all of your marketing materials. It truly provides that added personal touch that many need to encourage them to purchase from your business.

There are many ways that you can leverage video content for your brand, ranging from creating stories and live videos to uploading videos that you have pre-filmed in advance. All of these video forms help you get in front of your audience in their preferred manner and grow your business faster.

When it comes to stories or story-type sharing, Instagram, Facebook, and Snapchat are all great platforms for you to use. Instagram and Facebook offer stories that can be shared to your profile, whereas Snapchat is entirely built around story-type sharing. Each platform can be leveraged by creating unique, behind-the-scenes footage that allows you to share a relationship with your customers and followers that is more personal than a formal newsfeed. When you share your stories, make sure that everything you share is relevant and portrays your brand in the best way possible to avoid creating a story feed that detracts from your brand's quality and purpose.

Live video is another form of footage that you can use to grow your business with. Live video allows your customers to watch you and engage with you in real-time, making it feel as though you have a personal relationship with your audience. You can use live video to do Q&A calls, to do product demos, and to announce updates for your business while having a real-time conversation with your customers about whatever your live topic may be. The back-and-forth interaction makes this particular type of film both popular and successful, and you can use a live call-to-action to prompt people to buy from your business or otherwise take action that will lead them through your sales funnel.

Footage that you have already filmed is not quite as interactive as live content, but when it is designed and edited properly, it can be used for many different things. You can use this footage to share instructional videos, updates, and informational videos to your social media accounts. They can be uploaded as a post, or uploaded to YouTube and then shared as a post to your platform if you are going to be using YouTube as a part of your primary marketing strategy. Although you cannot get live comments, people can comment on your video depending on where it is posted, so be sure to take the time to comment back to people so that they still get that personalized feel. If you create and promote video content and then fail to respond to those who engage with you, you will miss out on a huge opportunity to really leverage that personal connection.

A great way to turn video marketing itself into a strategy that extends beyond cultivating brand awareness and into drawing traffic to your website is to create videos for YouTube and leverage them elsewhere on the net. YouTube videos can be created either with you talking and sharing information or with you doing a voiceover for an informative video that educates your audience on something relevant to your business. For example, if you are a business coach, your video could focus entirely on identifying your target audience and creating your "target persona" so that people watching your video learn how to clearly identify their own target audience.

After you have created this video, you can share it out to Facebook and promote it as an advertisement, as well as send it out to your email list. This way, when people see the video, not only do they receive high-value content right then and there, but they also receive an incentive or reason to further explore who your brand is and what you have to offer.

These days, some brands are even promoting their videos at the beginning of YouTube videos so that when people are looking for similar content, they come across their video first. This is a great way to capture your target audience and provide them high value while also encouraging them to follow you and pay attention to you, rather than having them instead click through to your competitor and purchase from them. Using this strategy correctly can have massive benefits, so it is definitely worth looking into.

Do Create a Strong Facebook Presence

Facebook continues to serve as one of the best platforms to grow your business when it comes to creating a social media presence. If you are going to pick just one platform to grow your business on, pick Facebook. Facebook is a powerful business tool for many reasons, but one of the most important reasons is that people will frequently go to Facebook to verify the quality of business before actually buying anything from that business. Facebook allows people to see what type of content business posts, how frequently they update their business page, and whether or not the reviews for that particular business are of high quality. They can also see what is being said about the business, or to the business, through the comments section of your posts.

When it comes to growing your business online, Facebook offers great in-app features as well as ones that can be integrated with Instagram, which is a social media platform that is also owned by Facebook. Some of these features include pages that have shoppable content, the ability to tag your products so that people can go straight to the product page on your website, and customer service features such as chat through messenger. Facebook also offers an extensive and proven native advertising opportunity that allows you to promote advertisements on Facebook and Instagram so that you can get your products or services in front of users scrolling the app. This particular paid advertising feature allows you to increase your viewership without having to do quite so much hard work with your organic advertisements.

Creating a Facebook page should be one of the first things that you focus on when you launch your business online, and it should be a platform that you seek to maintain. Keeping a consistent, updated page is important in keeping your brands' credibility and growing your business online. If you do not want to upload to your page consistently, you can always automate your content so that you only need to create and schedule content once per week or once per month, rather than uploading new content every day.

Do Start Your Own Blog

Blogging is an important tool to leverage when it comes to online marketing. If you want to grow your business rapidly, and get more traffic to your website, you need to use your website to host a blog that is relevant to your business and industry. Creating a blog helps give people more reason to visit your website, offers you more unique reasons to promote your website freshly consistently, and also makes your website easier for people to find.

When it comes to blogging, you can leverage your posts to position yourself as an expert in your industry by writing content that educates and informs people on topics that are relevant to your niche. For example, if you are in the food industry with custom desserts being your niche, you could have an entire blog focused on topics relating to creating custom desserts. This could include DIY techniques for people who want to try it themselves, updates on the latest trends in custom desserts, and reviews on products that you have tried when it comes to making custom desserts. All of these topics are relevant to your niche while also providing you with great content to update your blog with. Then, not only are you creating fresh new content for your audience, but you are also creating a fresh new opportunity for you to drive your audience to your website consistently.

In addition to allowing you to regularly drive more traffic to your website through organic marketing, blogging also improves your ability to leverage search engine optimization, or SEO, to get more traffic to your website from search engines. When you blog, you upload more content to your website that is filled with keywords that your audience is likely to be searching on platforms like Google, which means that Google is going to be more likely to display your website over any other. As a result, you will get more organic traffic through search engines, too, which means that you will have an additional source of traffic landing on your website.

Do Take Advantage of Email Marketing

Email marketing, as you will grow to understand, is one of the most powerful forms of marketing available on the internet today. As you will learn more about in Chapter 6: A License to Make Money: Your List, your email list is the only thing that you truly own on the internet, aside from your domain. Without your list, you do not have any guaranteed way to contact your audience so that you can increase your sales.

Beyond giving you a guaranteed way to contact your audience, email marketing is still one of the best ways to contact your audience with new updates and offers in your business. Plus, you can customize and design your emails in a way that perfectly brands them to your business and makes it even easier for you to build brand recognition as you go. Since we will be talking in-depth about email marketing later, I am not going to go too deep into specifics right now, but understand that email marketing is definitely something you should do in your business. No matter what you may perceive its reputation to be, it is a powerful solution for any business that wants to generate greater sales.

Learn How to Produce High-Quality Copy

When you are an online marketer, producing high-quality copy is crucial if you will have people actually stop to pay attention to your brand. Without high-quality copy material, people are unlikely to pay attention to your business because what you have written is uninteresting, difficult to read, or laid out in a way that makes it unappealing to your audience. As a result, you are going to have a hard time capturing the attention of your audience and converting them into customers who are ready to purchase from your business.

What you need to do to create a high-quality copy ultimately depends on where that copy is being shared. Copy on a static website page, for example, is going to have different requirements from a copy on a social media post. That being said, every form of copy can be held to certain standards that can ensure that it has been properly designed to capture attention and produce results for you and your brand.

The first thing you need to do when it comes to writing any copy is to research the method that the copy is being delivered through. Whether you are writing a blog post, a social media caption, Amazon product descriptions, or website copy, stop and do some research to see how each form of copy is supposed to be laid out to produce the highest quality of results. Some forms of the copy will require headers and body content, whereas others will require a basic one to two sentences to get the message across. Knowing what is required for the form of copy that you are creating is important, as it will help you design yours properly.

Next, you need to make sure that the topic of your copy is relevant and interesting to your customers. When it comes to writing about topics that your customers are interested in, you need to consider both the content itself and the way that you present the content to make sure that it is a topic that captures your readers' interest and keeps it. You can get a feel for what topics keep your readers' interest by paying attention to what popular bloggers and influencers in your industry are talking about. Even if you are not a blogger or influencer, the topics that the bloggers and influencers in your industry are talking about are likely to be trending topics that you can leverage for your own copy.

After you have created your copy, you need to make sure that you proofread it. You want a copy that is free of spelling and grammatical errors, as well as a copy that features language that your customers understand. In other words, you need to be using the slang that is relevant to your customer base so that they understand what you are talking about and relate to what you have said.

After you have completed these elements of your copy, you are ready to publish it. The next step comes after you have already published it when you check in on the analytics around the copy a few hours and days later to see how it performed. Keeping an eye on your copy's performance helps you spot trends in what types of copy your customers like most, which helps you decide what to write, and how, when it comes to creating copy for the future.

Chapter Summary

Because of how long online marketing has been around for, there are countless pieces of advice and guidance that can be offered to help new marketers, like you, grow successful more rapidly than ever before. Although trial and error still matter toward growing your own business, as it gives you the value of hands-on experience, learning from others is powerful, too. As you grow your own business, make sure you do not obsess over other marketers, sell low ticket items, or get stuck in a game of perfectionism causing you to stand still. Remember, good enough is good enough and it is perfectly fine to leave room for growth so that you can do even better in the future.

When it comes to things that you should do, you absolutely should leverage video content, get your business on Facebook, start your own blog, and take advantage of email marketing. Although the latter three are sometimes referred to as "out of date" in certain industries, this is more of a buzz topic than anything else. People love to declare that certain types of marketing are "dead" when, in reality, they are still alive and thriving. This is done in an effort to generate buzz, get more clicks, and attempt to be "ahead of the market." In reality, these methods are still massively successful and worth the effort for you to generate a business that will provide you with great results in the long run. You should certainly go for it and leverage these strategies to get more traffic to your business and buying your products so that you can generate a larger amount of profit in less time.

Chapter 4: Positioning

*"Content builds relationships.
Relationships are built on trust.
Trust drives revenue."*
— Andrew Davis

Your positioning in the market can be viewed as the equivalent of your reputation in the market, and it is an important element of your business. Although you cannot entirely control your position in the market, you can influence certain elements of your position that can help you lock in your desired position in the market. Doing this allows you to be seen the way that you want to be seen, which earns you countless benefits, including perceived value, perceived reputation, and perceived popularity and credibility. In this chapter, you will understand what positioning is, why you need it, and how you can leverage your own positioning in your business. As a result, you will be able to identify and cultivate your own reputation and, hopefully, lock that reputation through a specific marketing strategy designed to help you.

What Positioning Is and Why You Need It

Positioning is the practice of attempting to occupy a certain part of the market with a specific impression or reputation that your customers will come to know you as. For example, Adidas is presently developing the positioning of being an eco-friendly brand that will be exclusively using recycled plastics by 2024. Virtually every brand engages in positioning, one way or another, whether they realize it or not. As with anything in business, being aware of what it is that you are doing allows you to identify your goal and then take logical steps toward bringing that goal to life.

When it comes to growing an online business, identifying your positioning should be one of your primary goals so that you can incorporate it into your marketing plan. Without a clear idea of what your positioning is going to be, it can be challenging for you to know exactly what marketing strategies will be most effective in helping you reach your goals.

Positioning is not only going to help you establish and work toward marketing goals, but it is also going to give you another massive benefit when it comes to running your business. You will have the opportunity to have a complete guideline for you to run your business based on the reputation that you want to establish. This means that you will have guidelines for what types of products or services you should be selling, what price points you should be selling at, where you should be selling, and who you should be selling to. You will also access a guideline for how your brand should look, feel, and sound, what involvement you should have in your community, and what you should be doing to build your community around you. With the right positioning in mind, you can completely outline the path toward your success with very little effort.

Positioning Is Not a Guarantee

Despite how much effort you can put into your positioning, it is important for you to know that positioning is not a guarantee. When you work toward positioning your business, you are creating the foundation for an ideal reputation or perception to be made regarding your business. That being said, how your business is actually going to be perceived really depends on how your customers actually feel about your brand and what messages they take away from what you have shared. There are also other factors, such as where you sit in relevance to your competition, that can change the actual position that you hold in the market.

In some cases, you will not be able to change certain impressions that you have made, nor are you going to adjust your positioning quickly. You might find that rather than entering straight into your desired position, you find yourself sitting elsewhere in the market instead. In this case, you can do the best with what you have and continue to work toward securing your desired position until you reach it. Or, if you are happy with the position you end up in, such as if you find unexpected profitability that exceeds what you were aiming for, you can adapt your plan to fit this new position.

Although you cannot fully control your position, you can use feedback from your customers and your audience to help you identify where your position currently is and what you can do to adjust it. By using feedback and analytics to help you gauge where you are and determine a logical and reasonable strategy to advance toward where you want to go, you can take back some control and grow your business in your chosen direction. You will learn more about how to do this in the "Receiving Feedback About Your Position" and "Managing Your Position in the Market" sections below.

Positioning Through Your Brand Identity

Positioning with your brand identity comes through creating a brand that *looks* like it should fit in a certain part of the market. When it comes to branding, aesthetics is everything as they provide you with the opportunity to design a first impression that ultimately paves the way for what people think of when they see your brand in the first place.

The first part of creating your brand is determining what general image you are going with, and what colors you will accompany that general image with. For example, you might have a sleek, modern image with clean straight lines paired with the colors black, white, and navy blue to showcase that you are a professional brand. Alternatively, you might have a sleek, modern image with clean straight lines paired with white, pink, and purple to show that you are a modern, feminine brand. The specific image and colors that you combine can say a lot about who you are and where you want to fit into the market, so it is important that you pick the right combination for your brand.

Once you have picked your general image, you want to get clear on the more specific parts of your image, such as what types of photographs you are going to feature. This includes what and who will be in the photographs, where they will be taken, and how they will be styled. Again, the actual content and context of your photography can play a huge role in how your brand is perceived, so you need to start creating an image that is specific to the reputation that you desire to have. For example, if you have a professional general image coupled with pictures of people wearing suits and using the latest technology or sleek images of the latest technology, people will immediately know that you are selling technology. Alternatively, if you have a feminine image coupled with women wearing feminine clothes such as dresses and head wraps, people will assume that you are a fashion company. Make sure that the context and content of your images accurately line up with what you are marketing so that people know what to expect with your brand. If they do not line up for any reason whatsoever, you might confuse your customers and drive traffic away from your website, rather than toward your sales.

Finally, you need to include the actual wording linked to your brand. This includes your brand name, headings on your website, bios on your social media platforms, and actual written content that you feature on your website and elsewhere on the net. When it comes to positioning, your written content offers you the opportunity to fill in the gaps by providing specific details as to who you are, what you have to offer, and what part of the market you are aiming to occupy. Make sure that you use the right vocabulary and tone to convey the reputation that you want to have so that you are speaking your way into success with your brand.

Positioning Through Your Products and Services

After your brand has been identified and positioned, you need to position your products and services. When it comes to positioning, it is not enough to just pick out products that fit into your particular niche and consider the process "done." Instead, you need to make sure that every single product or service that you choose to promote says something about your business, particularly toward the reputation that you want to cultivate for yourself.

The key areas that you need to consider on your products or services include what they offer, how they look, and the quality that they possess. You want products that help you define exactly what you desire your reputation to be, and where you are positioned in the market.

For example, if you want to be seen as the best brand to go to for offering the latest cutting-edge technology, you need to constantly be updating your store with content that is actually cutting edge and updated. If you were to attempt to portray this message, yet your products were always outdated, you would destroy the integrity of your brand and become known as being the business that did *not* have what they said they had. Likewise, if you said you had the trendiest clothes in stock, yet you were a season or two behind, or your clothes were nowhere near the latest trends, you would receive the same reputation.

Keeping your store stocked with products or services that resemble exactly the image that you are building through your branding is important. Not only will this help you with anchoring in the exact position that you are looking for, but it will also help you stay in integrity with the brand that you are cultivating for your business. This is important, as integrity is a large part of what makes brands trustworthy, which in turn increases their sales and profitability.

Positioning Through Your Price Points

Your price points are another part of your business that can be leveraged to help you anchor in the exact position that you want to have in your business. When it comes to positioning through your price points, the way that you leverage this tool is fairly simple: you price according to how you want to be perceived.

If you want your brand to be perceived as a bargain value brand or one that is going to offer the best deals and discounts, you always want to price lower than the average pricing out there for every product you offer. If you are aiming to have a bargain brand, you want to make sure that you do not price *too* low, as part of your marketing strategy will likely revolve around having frequent deals, discounts, and coupons made available to further promote the idea that you have the lowest prices out there. If you price too low from the jump, you will not be able to use these additional savings to increase your perceived image as having the lowest prices out there.

If you want your brand to be perceived amongst the average brands out there, including the ones who are selling around average prices, you should price your products or services as close to the middle of the range of pricing for your industry. This way, you are seen on-par with other brands in your industry, and you are positioning yourself directly amongst them. In most cases, the "middle of the way" is the default setting for brands when it comes to pricing, as this puts you in the category of the majority. If you do not want to be perceived as cheap or as too expensive and out of reach, this is the right place for you to position your brand in terms of pricing.

If you want to be perceived as a high-value brand with the best possible products and services available on the market, you will want to price your products or services on the upper end of the scale. Setting your prices higher than the average market price, coupled with an elite-style brand, is the best way to increase the perceived value of your business and increase your potential profits from your company. Note that this is not the only way to make high ticket sales, but it can certainly make turning high ticket sales much easier as your entire image is perceived as much higher quality than virtually any other brand out there.

When it comes to positioning through pricing, you also need to look at your competition and see how they are pricing. What seems low, medium, or high to you might not be accurate to what is actually low, medium, or high in the market. Pay attention to the brands that inspire you and that you want to be recognized amongst and price accordingly.

Positioning Through Your Location

Positioning through your location is another great opportunity for you to let people know who you are and what they can expect from your brand. Although you cannot position yourself by physically placing yourself amongst the brands that you want to be seen amongst, you can still position yourself by picking the spots that you will be marketing online accordingly.

On the internet, every form of marketing positions you among a certain crowd and creates a certain image for your brand that will contribute to how you are perceived by your audience. It is important that you research each platform and the reputation that it carries so that you know exactly what that particular platform might be saying about you and your brand. Ideally, you want to be using the platforms that help you position yourself in front of your audience while also cultivating the right message for your brand. For example, if you are selling large quantities of products, you might want to position yourself on Amazon and social media as a way for you to get your brand in front of your customers. Alternatively, if you are selling someone else's products as an influencer, you might want to leverage a platform like Instagram and Twitter, where engagement and conversion ratios tend to be higher. Choosing the right placement will ensure that you are getting seen by the right audience and that you are giving off the right message about who your brand is and what you have to offer.

Positioning Through Your Marketing Strategy

The final part of your business that you can leverage for positioning is your marketing strategy. The marketing strategy that you choose to employ with your business says a lot about your brand, as this is how you decide to actually promote your products and services. When it comes to this, you can be seen as selective, casual, enjoyable, pushy, overwhelming, excited, tacky, sleazy, or any other number of things based on the strategies that you choose to use. Naturally, you want to choose the marketing strategy that will help you create the right image for yourself and your brand.

When it comes to positioning through your marketing strategy, the best thing that you can do is follow the guideline that you have set out for yourself by following the previous steps for positioning your business. By incorporating these elements into your marketing strategy, you can design a strategy that creates the exact image you want for your brand while effectively getting your business in front of your audience.

After you have made your strategy, you can compare it to your desired positioning and see how it holds up to the image that you are trying to create. If you notice that your strategy is out of integrity with your desired image at any given point, adapt it as needed to ensure that your marketing strategy also serves your branding and positioning. This way, you can feel confident that every element of your strategy will help you anchor into the position that you desire to occupy in the marketplace.

Receiving Feedback About Your Position

As I previously mentioned, you cannot guarantee your position in any industry, the best you can do is create a strong strategy to help you get into that position and hope that the market responds to you by putting you in that particular position. That being said, there is no way to tell whether or not you have achieved that positioning other than through listening to what people are saying about you and your brand.

At first, receiving feedback on your brand, especially relating to your position, will be challenging because you will have to establish yourself enough to warrant feedback. In this case, you will have to get creative and focus on paying attention to who is responding to your content. Ideally, your target audience should be the primary ones who are liking your content and following your page early on. You may not be getting much engagement beyond these basics in the beginning, but paying attention to it can help you determine if you are on the right track or not.

As people begin to purchase from you, you will begin to receive further feedback. You can also pay attention to who furthers their engagement with your brand by opting into your e-newsletter, commenting on your content, or purchasing your products. As this happens, you can also encourage feedback by engaging in dialogue with your followers and customers and by following up with those who purchase from you. The more that you encourage this type of feedback, the better you will be able to determine where you are positioned in the market. This way, you can tell whether or not your strategies have been successful in getting you into the position that you desire to occupy.

Managing Your Position in the Market

As you continue to grow your business, you need to manage your position in the market. This means that you may need to adapt your strategy as you go to push yourself closer into your desired position, or if you have already reached it, you will simply need to monitor your analytics to ensure that you maintain it. When it comes to positioning, reaching your desired position once does not mean that you are guaranteed to stay there forever. Remember: new brands are always popping up, and some of them are bound to want to get into the same position that you have. If you are not working toward maintaining your position, you will be pushed right out of the way by your competitors, which could result in a serious threat to the success of your business.

Managing your position and adjusting your position as needed is simple: you will hear about exactly what you need to do in the feedback that you receive from your audience. Pay attention to what they are saying and what it says in reference to where you are trying to position yourself and adapt your strategy accordingly. For example: if you want to run a bargain brand and find that people are saying that the quality is as cheap as your prices and makes buying from you not worth it, you know that you need to start purchasing from higher quality sources. Another example is if you are trying to position yourself as high end, but you are being told that your products are too expensive, you may need to adjust who you are marketing toward. You might be marketing toward customers who cannot afford your prices, meaning that you cannot earn profits from this particular part of the market.

Receiving feedback from your customers, along with adjusting your strategies accordingly is a normal part of running a business. This will be relevant not only to your positioning but also to your marketing strategies as a whole. The more feedback you receive directly through your customers and analytics, the more you will be able to grow your business.

Chapter Summary

Positioning is a term that refers to what part of the market you want to occupy with your business. Choosing your position in the market ultimately requires you to decide what you want your reputation to be and who you want to be known as in your industry. After you have chosen who you want to be known as in your industry, you can use this as a goal to help you determine which marketing strategies are going to help you create this desired reputation and position.

You can incorporate positioning strategies into your marketing strategy through what brand identity you choose, which products or services you sell, how you price your products or services, what location you choose, and what marketing strategy you use. When it comes to positioning your brand, you will always need to work toward maintaining your position because industries are ever-changing. New people are always coming up and building brands in your industry, and if you are not keeping yourself on +top, you will be pushed out of the way by someone who was more diligent than you were. If you find that you never reached your desired position in the first place, you can leverage analytics and consumer feedback to create a new strategy that will lead you to where you want to go.

Chapter 5: No Traffic, No Money

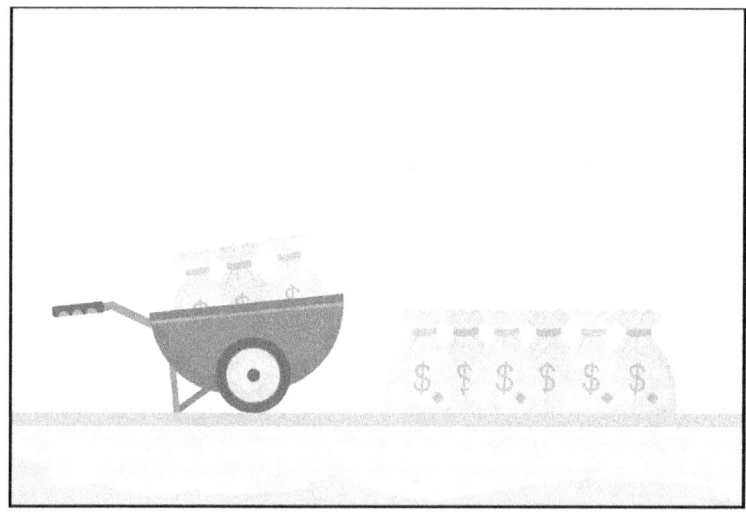

"Sell-sell-sell sales methods simply do not work on social media."
— *Kim Garst*

It might seem obvious that if you do not have any traffic coming into your business, you do not have any money coming into your business, either. When it comes to generating sales in your business, you need to have a steady flow of customers landing on your website and purchasing your products; otherwise, you will never make any sales in your business. As a result, you will not have a business but rather an expensive and time-consuming hobby.

Generating traffic can be done in multiple ways, but one of the most effective ways that you can do it is through paid advertising. Paid advertising is more consistent and brings greater results than virtually any other strategy as it achieves far greater and more consistent reach than any form of organic marketing that is available to you. The key to getting the most out of paid online marketing is knowing what you are doing and creating advertisements with the right design and the right demographics plugged in. This way, you can reach your target audience with content that will be likely to pique their interest. If you fall short on either part of this, you are going to find yourself struggling to achieve any results with your paid advertisements, which will render them useless.

How Paid Online Marketing Strategies Work

The internet shows two types of content to virtually everyone on it, no matter what platform you find yourself on. These two types include organic (unpaid) content and paid content. Organic content is every type of unpaid content that exists on the internet, whereas paid content is every advertisement, sponsored post, or other forms of paid promotional materials that you see floating around. No other form of content exists online.

Both types of content are held up to specific algorithms that determine what content is shown to who and when. These algorithms ultimately decide if the content is relevant enough for that individual and if they are likely to enjoy it based on what they are looking at or what site they are on. Certain sites, such as social media platforms, use your activity to determine what your interests are and show you posts that you are most likely to be interested in. Others, like search engines, take what you have searched and search for the most relevant content based on your search terms.

When it comes to organic content, you have to meet a large number of criteria to be seen as relevant or interesting by your target audience. As a result, you have a harder time getting seen and interacting with your audience. Furthermore, if someone is not directly following you or subscribed to your content, they are even less likely to see what you are posting because there are others who are competing for that same viewership. Lastly, if you are not consistently uploading new organic content, you find yourself quickly being covered up by other people who are creating newer, fresher content.

On the other hand, paid content is, well, *paid.* When you pay to advertise online, you are purchasing space on peoples' newsfeeds or search results for your posts to consistently be seen over an extended period of time. Unlike organic posts, yours will not have a "lifespan" that results in them no longer being seen after a few hours or days. Instead, they will continue to be promoted in the feed so long as you continue to keep the promotion active. In addition to having your post seen longer, you will also get seen by a larger audience of people because you will be promoted to more than just those who are following you or a select few who are looking for similar content. Instead, you will be promoted to everyone who fits your demographic and who is interested in the type of content you share. As a result, you have a much easier time reaching even more of your target demographic and increasing your sales through this particular strategy.

When it comes to marketing online, paid to advertise is crucial regardless of how much organic content you plan on using to get your brand in front of your audience. Even if you plan on using organic content daily, you are still going to need to leverage paid content so that you can maximize the flow of traffic coming through to your website to purchase your products. If you fail to implement paid online marketing, you are leaving massive amounts of money on the table in your business.

Leveraging Facebook Ads to Land Leads

Facebook is one of the best platforms to run your business through, and this remains true when it comes to paid advertisements, too. With Facebook, you can pay to promote advertisements on both Facebook and Instagram simultaneously. Through these paid promotions, you can boost your content up in the native feed of everyone who follows your page, plus everyone who fits your target demographic. This way, as people scroll through their newsfeeds, they come across your content as a part of all of the other content that already exists on their feed by their friends and other brands they follow.

When it comes to Facebook, in particular, there are three types of advertisements that you can use: boosted posts, time-sensitive campaigns, and ongoing campaigns. All three show up natively in the newsfeed and provide the same general aesthetic and options but run for different reasons and with different time lengths. As well, they are all used for different purposes when it comes to advertising your products on Facebook or Instagram.

Boosted posts are a form of promotion introduced by Facebook that allows you to pay to promote a post that has already been performing well on your page. This is a great opportunity to take a piece of content that you have already proven as being popular and interesting and promote it to others in your target audience so that they can find you, too. Promoting this type of content helps you get more out of organic content that is performing well, while also being far more likely to get positive results with your promotion. Beyond that, the existing likes and comments on your post prove that it is popular and helps break the ice for people who come across your sponsored post.

When you choose to boost a post on Facebook (or Instagram), the only thing you have to do is click "boost post" and then choose your audience, the length of the boost, and how much money you want to spend on the advertisement. You can pick either a daily or an overall budget for your advertisement to help you get it in front of your audience. When it comes to who your exact demographic is, you should outline the demographic that fits your exact target audience. If you are not entirely sure as to who that is, you can always try split testing. Split testing can be done on any form of a paid marketing campaign and allows you to set up a few different advertisements with different demographics. This helps you identify which demographic interacts most with your posts and is most likely to convert into sales. Running a few split tests early on can help you find out exactly who to market to later on, allowing you to get the most out of your marketing budget in future campaigns.

Time-sensitive campaigns are campaigns that are scheduled to appear for a specific amount of time. For example, if you are running a promotion from Monday to Friday in a specific week, you might create an advertisement that runs from Monday to Friday and then expires. These types of advertisements can be made in your Facebook ad manager, and are simple to create using Facebook's guided process. You simply go to your manager, choose which type of campaign you want to create and what the goal of your campaign is. While there are several options to choose from, the easiest and most effective one to use for online marketing is the goal that gets more traffic landing on your website.

After you have chosen your goal, you can work on your ad creative consisting of the images and text related to your advertisement. It is important that you choose the right images and text to go with your advertisement to entice peoples' interest and encourage them to actually follow through with the call to action associated with your advertisement. Again, split testing is a great idea early on as this helps you identify which types of graphics and captions your audience responds to best. Once you know, you can go with the trend that works and continues to improve the quality and results of your ads over time.

Next, you need to outline your demographic and your budget. This part is exactly the same as it is with boosted campaigns. You can choose the demographic that fits your target audience and set your budget either based on your daily spending budget or your total spending budget. With a time-sensitive advertisement, this budget will only count for the duration of the advertisement, and then it will be done.

The alternative to time-sensitive advertisements is evergreen or ongoing campaigns. These campaigns have no expiry date and run until you decide to shut them off. You should not use this form of the campaign until you have seen success in low-budget time-sensitive campaigns so you can feel confident that you are only marketing to the exact audience that fits your business. Once you have accumulated successful results and important analytics from your smaller campaigns, you can run an ongoing campaign as an opportunity to continually get in front of your audience. In fact, you should actually run 3-5 ongoing campaigns to get as much traffic to your business as you can. This way, you have plenty of advertisements driving traffic your way and increasing your chances of making sales.

When you do run an ongoing campaign, the budget works slightly differently as well. Unlike time-sensitive campaigns which have a budget that expires when the campaign does, the ongoing campaign has a budget that is relevant to a set period of time and renews as long as the advertisement remains active. This budget can either be set for daily amounts or monthly amounts. Either one works, you can pick whichever one suits your budget needs best so that you get the best results from your advertisements.

Leveraging Facebook campaigns effectively can help you create massive success in driving more traffic to your website, as long as you are using the right strategies at the right times. This means that boosted posts should only be used when content has performed well, as boosting content that has not performed well organically is unlikely to perform well as paid content, either. Time-sensitive offers should only be used for time-sensitive deals, or as a way to test the market to see which types of advertisements perform best in your industry. If you are using them as a test, make sure that you monitor them closely and shut them off if they are not performing well so that you do not spend unnecessary money on your advertisements. Ongoing campaigns should be used for something that will be ongoing or generic in your business so that you can feel confident that the content will not expire, leaving you advertising something outdated to your customers. As long as you are promoting evergreen content, however, ongoing campaigns can keep a steady flow of traffic coming into your business every single month, earning you even more sales over time.

Other Social Media Paid Advertising Strategies

Facebook is not the only platform that has paid advertisements that you can take advantage of. As aforementioned, Instagram also has a great platform that is powered through the state-of-the-art Facebook platform. As well, Twitter, YouTube, and Pinterest also feature excellent paid advertisement opportunities that allow you to improve your visibility and get seen by a larger portion of your audience.

Most social media platforms are fairly similar in how they function. Each one offers a guided system that helps walk you through the process of designing your ad creative and determining who your demographics are so that you can advertise to the right people. Furthermore, you can also use split testing on each platform to see which types of content perform best on each platform. You should note that different types might perform better on different platforms, so do not assume that just because you have it figured out on one means that you have it figured out on both. Take the time to research and understand each unique platform to ensure that you are getting the best results on every single one.

When it comes to spending your ad budget on social media platforms, it is obvious that you want to advertise on the ones that you are actually active on. This way, if people like your brand, they can follow you and gain more access to your organic content, which will improve your visibility and ratings. It also gives you more people to advertise to in order to organically drive traffic to your website.

Beyond this obvious fact, however, here are some statistics to help you decide what platforms to advertise on:

- Instagram generated advertisers more than $7 billion in mobile ad revenue
- 80% of people on Twitter will visit your website; its audience converts incredibly well
- On YouTube, you only pay if someone watches your advertisement for more than 30 seconds, so you do not pay for any lead beyond those that are actually likely to convert
- Pinterest averages $4.30 revenue for every $1 spent on advertising

The Power of Google Paid Advertisements

Outside of social media, there is an entirely separate paid advertisement platform that you can leverage known as Google Paid Advertisements. Google advertisements are actually the ones that power YouTube advertisements, so if you get involved with sharing advertisements on YouTube, you will already be set up for sharing advertisements on Google.

Google advertisements can be used to advertise your brand on the search engine itself, or you can choose to display your advertisements with Google's partners. For example, when you visit a blog and see advertisements for certain brands or products along the side of that blog, chances are placed there by Google and the brands who work with Google.

Running advertisements on Google is easy and can lead to a massive return on your investment, as Google is used by a massive portion of the population. To date, Google continues to be the most popular search engine, making it one of the best choices to advertise with. That being said, you will need to have a strong understanding as to who your target audience is when it comes to launching an advertisement on Google to ensure that your ad budget pays off by reaching the right people.

After you have done some research on who your target audience is and have verified them through smaller advertisements, you can begin to run advertisements on Google and feel confident that your advertisements will pay off. When you are ready, you can use the following steps to launch an advertisement on Google to help you drive more traffic to your website and increase your sales.

The first thing that you need to do is sign up, which can easily be done by going to Google AdWords and signing up for your account there. After you have set up your account, Google will immediately take you to the page titled "Your first campaign" and will help you start setting up your advertisement.

Before you do anything else, you are going to need to set a budget for your advertisement. You should define a daily budget for your advertisement to ensure that you never go over your spending limits, as not setting your budget could lead to a very costly mistake. When it comes to setting your budget, the best starting budget is typically around $5 per day. This way, you can start working with Google and getting a feel for how the analytics work as well as how much traffic is being driven to your site through your advertisements. Once you get a feel for how your advertisements are working, you can increase your daily spending budget to match whatever investment you feel that you can comfortably invest in your Google ads.

The next part of creating your Google ad is setting your target audience. Just like with social media advertising, you want to get as specific about your target demographic as you can so that they are the ones that will see your advertisement.

Next, you need to choose what network you are going to use for your advertisement. This is where you can decide if you want your advertisement to be posted in line with search results, or displayed on Google's partner websites. If you choose "Search Network" as your option, you are going to have your advertisement show up anywhere that the Google search engine is used to conduct searches online. If you choose "Display Network" as your option, your content will be shown on blogs and Google partners as a display advertisement for people to engage with.

After you have chosen how you want your ad to show up, you need to choose what your keywords are. Keywords offer Google the opportunity to make sure that it is showing your advertisement to relevant users, so it is important that you choose keywords that are relevant to your brand and what you are promoting with your advertisement. You should use around 15-20 keywords for your advertisement so that anytime these keywords are searched on Google, as long as your advertisement is relevant, it is likely to be shown to the individual searching. Google has a built-in keyword tool that you can use on this step to help you pick keywords and verify whether or not they are strong enough to help your advertisement get seen.

Now, you need to write the content for your ad. You want to keep your ad short and simple, as most people scrolling on Google or Google's partners are not going to read a long-winded excerpt about your business or your promotion. Furthermore, Google may not show the entire excerpt, which could drastically reduce the results of your advertisement. You want to make sure that you use a strong and enticing headline, a direct message, and a clear call to action to encourage people to take action on your ad. This will make it easier for your advertisement to get the message across and convert results. Let your website or the landing page that viewers will land on, be the page that gives more in-depth information about what you have promoted in your advertisement, as people who click through will be more likely to read the added content that you have provided.

Lastly, you need to create your ad! This happens simply through tapping the "save" button and then confirming your business and your payment options with Google. Once this is done, Google will charge you either within 30 days, or when your ad budget has been exhausted.

Chapter Summary

Although organic (unpaid) advertising is important to create a consistent brand for your business, it is not the most effective in reaching new customers and driving traffic to your website. If you want to earn sales through your business, you will need to use paid advertising as a way to maximize the volume of traffic landing on your website for you to sell to.

Paid advertisements can be done on virtually any social media platform or Google. Although other paid platforms do exist, these are the most effective at getting your brand put directly in front of your audience and creating strong conversion ratios. For that reason, you should favor these platforms over any other platform out there. When it comes to creating paid advertisements, it is important that you know exactly who your demographic is and what type of creative captures their attention best. This way, you can feel confident that the advertisements you create are going to have an impact. If you are not entirely sure, start out by split testing your campaigns with smaller budgets. You can split-test by creating two separate advertisements that either have the same audience but a different ad creative, or the same ad creative but two different audiences. Ad testing can help you generate analytics around who is likely to respond to your brand so that you can begin to use this information to create new ads going forward. As you continue to accumulate analytics surrounding which exact demographic is responding best to your ads and what creative they like best, you can use this information to create even stronger and more effective advertisements. Ideally, you should keep advertisements running at all times so that you have a steady flow of traffic, consistently making their way to your website. This way, you have a higher chance of turning conversions and making sales with your brand.

Chapter 6: A License to Make Money – Your List

"Not viewing your email marketing as content is a mistake."
— Chris Baggot

We had already discussed the importance of an email list previously when you learned how to make a basic sales funnel for your online business. Now, however, we will go into greater depth about the value of an email list, why you need one, and how you can create and nurture an email list so that you are more likely to gain benefits from this particular online marketing strategy.

What an Email List Affords You

You already have a strong idea surrounding the value of an email list, so I do not want to go into excessive detail about what you gain when you have one. That being said, let's recap the benefits that you gain from an email list so that you recall exactly why they are so important and why you should create one (even if you don't want to).

First things first, email subscribers are more likely to be buyers because they are committed enough to your brand to be willing to let you personally contact them through their email box. Most customers will think twice before giving their email away to a brand because they know that they are going to receive emails from that brand, so they have to really be interested in receiving further communications to actually sign up.

As well, aside from your website, you really only have control over your email list. Other forms of marketing, such as social media, can be taken away or altered and made it more challenging for you to take advantage of.

Your website and your email list will always remain in your control. However, this is perfect as you already know that you can create a strong sales funnel using just an email list and your website, which means that no matter what happens anywhere else online, you can still drive sales to your business.

Another great benefit with email is that it is an easy way to keep in touch with your audience and give them updates about your business. With social media, it is not guaranteed that everyone who follows you will see your posts. If they are the type of person who does not check their platforms frequently, chances are they do not even see your content at all. In fact, lately, most platforms only show content to about 10% of your followers. Unless your content gets a strong engagement, it is never seen by any additional followers, which results in you having a hard time getting your brand out there in front of your audience and making sales. With your email list, however, everyone who is subscribed receives your email, which means that there is no discrimination in how many people see what you have sent them. In other words, they are guaranteed to see the email. Whether or not they read it, however, ultimately depends on how effective you are when it comes to writing strong headlines and emails that are worth opening time and again.

How to Use Your Email List in Marketing

When it comes to using your email list in marketing, it is not effective enough to simply hoard emails and keep them "just in case" something terrible happens to the social media networks that you have grown your brand on. Instead, you want to incorporate these emails into an important part of your marketing and branding so that you can reach people in yet another way. Remember: you want to have as many "incoming" elements to your sales funnel as you possibly can to ensure that you reach the most sales possible.

To use email marketing effectively, all you need to do is create a sales funnel that encourages people to sign up for your email list and then email your list every so often. Ideally, you should have a set schedule for when you are going to email your list so that they have content regularly coming into their inbox. This way, they come to expect the content that flows their way, and they are more likely to open your emails and see what you are sharing with them. Ideally, you should send emails anywhere from 1 to 5 times per week to ensure that you are getting enough content in the hands of your audience. It is important that when you write emails, you do not write them just to fulfill your content calendar and "get your name out there." In other words, if you have a business that produces a large amount of content and has plenty to talk about, you might consider sending out five emails per week. However, if your business only produces a small amount of new content, you might consider something like 1 or 2 times per week. It is important that every single email is full of high-value content so that when people receive the email, they know that it is worth opening and paying attention to. Having an email go out just for the sake of it, without really putting effort into strong content for the email, can result in you not achieving great results with your strategy. In the end, you might actually drive more people away than you attract through your email marketing strategy.

Growing Your Email List in 3 Easy Steps

Growing your email list has got to be one of the easiest strategies that you can put into effect, and can be fully automated, which makes it even easier. In fact, growing and nurturing your list can be done in as little as three easy steps and can continue to drive a large amount of traffic through to your business. Below, we will discuss what these three steps are so that you can create a strong email list strategy that both earns you several new email subscribers and nurtures your existing list effortlessly.

Step One: Create 6-12 Opt-In Freebies

As you may recall from chapter 2, some people use incentives to encourage people to sign up for their email list. This incentive could be anything from a free digital product download to a coupon code or anything else relating to your business that would appeal to you to your audience and encourage them to sign up for your email list. Incentives are an excellent tool to help get people on your list, allowing you to have even more people reach out through your emails.

A great way to leverage freebies or opt-in incentives is to create 6-12 of them ahead of time and alternate between them. Switching which freebie you are using every month or every other month gives people something new and fresh to look forward to, and it also gives you something new to the market to your audience. This way, rather than marketing the same freebie over and over, you can talk about a new one every so often, which encourages even more people to sign up.

Creating 6-12 freebies does not have to be challenging or time-consuming, and it is an excellent way to grow your list. To do so, set aside an afternoon or two of time where you can create either 6-12 different coupons for different products you sell, 6-12 digital downloads, or even 6-12 different small video clips or other incentives to encourage people to get on your list. If you are not entirely sure as to what you should be making, take a look at your competitors and see what they are offering to encourage people to opt-in to receive emails from them. Not only is this going to inspire you with new ideas, but it will also show you what types of freebies are most effective in your industry so that you can create stuff that your audience actually wants.

As you create your freebies, you might consider creating ones that coincide with any product launches, seasons, or holidays that may be relevant to your industry. Creating them to coincide with these particular occasions means that you have a coherent and consistent brand filled with plenty of great content for you to market to your audience.

Once you have created your freebies, you will want to update your autoresponder to have your current freebie available in the email that is automatically sent out when people sign up for your list. This way, they are getting the freebie that is actually being marketed to them, and not an outdated one. You will need to make sure that you upload your new freebie into the autoresponder each time the freebie changes so that you are always marketing and sending out the same freebie.

Step Two: Promote Your Freebies

Next, you need to start promoting your freebies. Since you have new freebies every month or every other month, you can easily use this as a talking point for you to drive more attention toward your email list. Simple social media updates or promotions saying "grab my latest freebie for a free ____!" or something similar is plenty to drive more attention to your email list. Although this type of promotion might not result in immediate sales since you are not driving people directly to products, you are giving yourself something new to talk about and promote while also getting people into your sales funnel. Once people are on your list, you can email them periodically to let them know about the latest sales and offerings, which can greatly improve your sales conversions.

When you promote freebies, it is important that you do so consistently. Do not think that just because you made one or two posts about your freebie immediately upon launching it that everyone who follows you on social media or your blog has now seen it. Understand that, as long as you are marketing properly, your follower count and blog readers are rapidly growing, and your brand is reaching the eyes of new people all the time. This means that you should be marketing your freebie each week, at least once per week, so that all of the people who are new to your brand can see your freebie and have the opportunity to get on your list. Staying consistent in this way will keep your list consistently growing, thus allowing you to have even more people to market to.

As you promote your freebies, it is important that you pay attention to what your audience is saying about the freebies that you are offering. Be sure to recognize which freebies gain the most attention, which ones gain the most engagement, and which ones are earning you the best sales conversions for your business. Understanding this gives you the opportunity to identify what your customers care about so that when you make offerings in the future, you can feel confident that they are ones that your audience is actually interested in purchasing.

Step Three: Send Out Regular E-Newsletters

After you have created your email list, you will have to engage with your list to make sure that people actually stay subscribed. Creating a list and then not nurturing it is a waste of your time, and it can result in people leaving your list because they forget that they even subscribed to your e-newsletter in the first place. Rather than being forgotten about and wasting your list, you should create a consistent schedule for your newsletters to go out on.

As I have already mentioned, you should be sending out a new e-newsletter at least 1-5 times per week to make sure that you are giving your subscribers plenty of content to read and engage with. This will also ensure that you stay fresh in their minds and that they are more likely to continue engaging with you elsewhere online and purchasing from your brand when they feel like purchasing what you are selling.

Each newsletter that you send out should be high quality and filled with value, not just marketing materials to encourage people to buy your products. Giving your readers more than just sales information gives them plenty more reasons to open your emails and see what you have sent them. This way, they know that even if they are not planning on buying from you, there is still plenty of reason for them to open your email and see what you have to say. Then, if they do happen to find a sale that they are interested in taking advantage of, they are likely to look into it and consider the purchase. All in all, if you give your readers more reason to read your emails beyond just the latest sales, you give your readers more reason to open your emails. As a result, they are more likely to see your latest sales and actually purchase from you.

Chapter Summary

Creating an email list is important for countless reasons. Not only is this one of the only things that you actually own in your online business, but it is also something that can easily be turned into a sales funnel to help you generate more traffic and sales in your business. Furthermore, emails are guaranteed to reach your customers' inboxes, which means that you are far more likely to get seen and generate traction through emails than you are through platforms like social media, where the algorithm can work against you at times.

To create a strong email list for your brand, you only need to engage in three steps: creating freebies, promoting freebies, and sending out regular e-newsletters. Freebies are designed to encourage people to sign up for your e-newsletter so that they actually get on your list. Creating 6-12 freebies gives you something new to promote every month or every other month so that you have fresh new reasons for why people should get on your list if they haven't already. Plus, it is a great opportunity for you to regularly turn attention toward your business and let people know what you have going on. Once you have gotten people on your list, you need to start sending out weekly emails to make sure that you are nurturing your list and making the most out of it. Growing a list without leveraging it to gain more sales is, ultimately, a missed opportunity.

Chapter 7: Online Marketing Is a Business

"Marketing is really just about sharing your passion."
— *Michael Hyatt*

Online marketing might be one of the easiest types of businesses to begin and run, but that does not make it any less of a business than, say, a brick-and-mortar retail store. When you run an online business, you need to be just as committed, clear, and strategic about running your business as any other business owner. Without the right mindset, perspective, and strategy, you will struggle to get your business out there in front of customers, and you will have an even harder time making any sales. In the end, if you are not approaching your business properly, you can easily find yourself completely missing the opportunity to succeed, and instead, fall flat on your face.

To help you take that next step toward success, we will discuss what you can do to help you take on the right approach and perspective when it comes to running your online marketing business. This way, you truly understand how to regard your business and grow it with intensity and intention, allowing you to generate as much success as you possibly can. Trust that by adjusting your perspective and taking the right approach to your business, you can make a massive shift in the level of success that you achieve with your brand.

You Need the Right Approach

When it comes to running an online marketing business, you need to understand the approach you take when running your business matters. If you approach your online marketing business with the expectation that you will be able to make an easy profit without any experience or understanding of what you are doing, you will fail. Pure and simple: online marketing is a business, and it requires you to approach your online marketing business with the same level of intention and intensity that you would approach any other form of business with. Instead of jumping online, making a random product or company website, and then throwing up some advertisements on various platforms, you need to take it seriously and do your research. You need to identify your niche so that you know exactly what types of products you are selling and why they are different from any other product on the market at this time. You need to identify your target audience and get clear on who they are and how you can talk to them so that you have someone to market your business to. You need to create a marketing strategy *on paper* that can be followed so that you always know what you need to be doing each day when you run your business. You need to make sure that your marketing plan matches your company goals and suits your audience in a way that is actually going to have an impact on reaching them and converting them into customers. You also need the willingness to actually follow up with your business by paying attention to consumer feedback and analytic reports to make sure that you have the impact that you desire to have with your business. If you are missing out on any of these steps, you will cost yourself money in the end, and you may even cost yourself your success.

Running an online marketing business takes effort, practice, and a clear understanding of what you are doing. Although anyone can learn how not everyone will succeed because not everyone is going to be willing to put in the work that it takes to do so. You want to come in, and you want to set yourself apart from the rest of the crowd by creating your business with knowledge and an understanding of what needs to happen for you to succeed. Believe it or not, in doing this, you will already have set yourself ahead of many others who are trying to generate the success that you are because you took your business seriously and others didn't.

With all this being said, understand that just because online marketing is not easy money does not mean that it cannot become easy money. Early on, it can be challenging as you have to educate yourself on new strategies and practices that you have likely never used before. As you continue to practice the strategies of online marketing and getting your business profitable, however, you will find that it becomes a lot easier because you learn how to do it. The steps in creating, growing, and selling your business will become even easier, and you will find that you have a lot more free time on your hands. As long as you are willing to endure the educational period and the learning curve that is required to get your business profitable, you will have an easy time making money with your online business. Chances are, you will even exceed your job-related earnings so that you can focus on your online marketing business as your primary income source.

You Must Start with a Budget

There seems to be a notion that if you start an online marketing business, you can do so with $0 and turn that into $100,000, $1 million, or more within a few months. This comes from a select few individuals who have started their businesses with $0 and generating that type of success for themselves and then telling everyone else that it is possible and that there is a specific way to do it. Although it certainly is possible, realize that most online marketing businesses will not have this same reality, and you need to be prepared for this fact. Rather than attempting to emulate these $0 to $1 million brands, which have a lot more going on behind the scenes than you know about, start your brand smart with a basic budget to help you invest in the right tools and advertisements to get yourself going.

Before I get into anything else, I want to give you the background on what it takes to truly make a business go from a $0 investment to $1 million in revenue. Aside from the few cases where the individual has zero experience but came up with an incredible idea and turned it into something massive, there are very few cases where the story depicted in the media is the truth. Even then, many of these businesses spent a great deal of time pitching to investors in order to gain the capital to create products or services for their customers or to otherwise get their brands out there. So, while they may have had $0 of their *own* money invested, they did have money invested in creating their businesses. Furthermore, those who truly had $0 likely also had massive amounts of failure, growth, and experience prior to getting into their businesses. Although their current business may have generated $1 million in a few months, chances are they failed several times and invested a lot of money into other businesses before reaching where they are now. They have likely invested a lot into their knowledge and understanding of online marketing, and so while their current business may have started with $0, they have probably invested way more than that in the past. In other words, what you read in the media is not always the full story, so do not attempt to compare yourself to these individuals, and do not let yourself be fooled by the idea that this is a smart way to launch your business.

Every single business need startup capital. The only difference is: online businesses typically require less startup capital than any other business out there because the cost of getting started is typically lower. You will need to set aside a budget to invest in things like a domain name, a basic website, an autoresponder for your emails, and advertisements. You may also want to have your own logo created, as well as graphics made for your website and your social media profiles so that your entire brand stays coherent and consistent. In all of these instances, you will require funds to invest so that you can actually make this happen. With that being said, you can always start with the most basic plans of the best tools that you can afford, and get your logos and graphics made from places like Fiverr or UpWork so that you do not have to pay an enormous fee for your branding materials. Still, you should anticipate that there will be investments, and you should prepare for those investments by having some startup funds available before you launch your business.

You Are Nothing Without a Profitable Market

A surprising number of brands are currently in the online space selling to markets that are not profitable. People who do not do their research and validate their brands often find themselves marketing to a niche that is non-existent, or that is too small to make a decent profit from. As a result, they find themselves investing money into creating and promoting a brand that never actually goes anywhere. Unfortunately, before they close up shop, many of these individuals decide to invest even more into promotional materials, as they attempt to generate some analytics that finds a profitable market in their niche.

What you can learn from this is simple: first, you need to make sure that you do plenty of research *before* launching your business to ensure that you are actually launching into a profitable market. You need to identify your niche and start looking for your possible clients online to get a feel for where they exist and how many of them there are. If you do not do this, you will find yourself facing the risk of marketing to too small or too large of an audience, both of which can be fatal to the success of your business. When it comes to researching your target audience, be thorough. Take your time and make sure that the audience both exists and is willing to pay for products or services like the ones you plan on marketing to them. If either of these is questionable or negative, you need to pick a new niche or a new product or service to promote. It is not worth it to take the risk with your business and find yourself launching into a market that will never earn you the profit that you seek. The second thing that you can learn from this is the importance of admitting if your business was flawed. Stubbornly increasing your marketing budget and attempting to find a market that is not there is only going to result in you wasting your money and your time. Instead, take the money that you would have invested in increased marketing efforts and begin a new venture, this time taking extra care in making sure that your market will be profitable. This way, you are not wasting your money, and you are improving your chances of generating a successful online marketing business.

If you are worried about what people will think of you if you fail, understand this: it is less foolish to quit something that was not working and use it as a lesson to create something that will than it is to stubbornly cling to something out of sheer pride. Not only will clinging to something out of pride result in you looking foolish to those around you, but it will also cost you large amounts of money, and it will waste your time. It can be challenging to admit when you have made a mistake or when something you thought would be a success flop, but this is a common reality in business. If you truly want to generate success, you can. You just have to be committed to taking every failure as a lesson to help you achieve success, rather than evidence that you should quit. If every business person quit because of a few troubles early on, the world would have virtually no economy because there would be no businesses to sustain it. Failure is inevitable, and for you, that should be seen as a positive thing because it means that any failure you may experience is just a part of the process.

You Need to Be Passionate About What You Do

If you have ever scrolled Instagram's discover tab for a few minutes, there is something that was likely painstakingly obvious to you as you did: there is a distinctive difference between brands who are passionate and brands who are not. Brands who are passionate about what they do have a very different image, message, and general feel from brands who are not passionate, and it can be seen just from a momentary glance at a few images on your mobile device.

Something that many new business owners do not understand about building a brand is that you are building an identity or a persona. Your brand needs a personality, an image, and a voice. What you are really creating is a "character" for your business that will interact with your audience, cultivate a sense of personality and charisma, and build relationships through trust and credibility. Your brand needs to be seen as something that can be interacted with, similar to how friends would interact, as this is what makes a brand feel enjoyable to be a part of and to associate with.

Brands that are not passionate about what they do struggle in virtually every way to create a personality that has a meaningful impact on the people who interact with them. They have a hard time creating a believable persona that allows them to engage in friendly relationships with their customers, and so people feel awkward and uncomfortable when they are communicating with that brand. Even if the brand has a well-orchestrated image, they will still have an awkward feel to them that makes it uncomfortable for people to engage and interact with them consistently. Most people won't even try, and those who do will rarely come back to the brand to continue building a relationship with it. Instead, people will choose to go to other brands where the personality is more believable and charismatic and more enjoyable to develop a relationship with.

In addition to struggling to create positive relationships with their customers, brands that lack passion for what they are doing also struggle to build a strong brand. Their lack of passion leads to a lack of effective and applicable knowledge around the niche they are serving, including for the customers and with the products or services themselves. These brands will have a hard time anticipating what products or services will fill the needs of their customers, and they will have a hard time understanding what the real needs of their customers are in the first place. Ultimately, they will not have a strong enough understanding or knowledge of what they are doing, which will lead to them not generating any level of success in their business.

For you, you want your brand to fall amongst those that are passionate. You want to have that easy ability to communicate with your customers, create products or services that fulfill their needs, and anticipate what is going to be successful and what is not going to be. This will not only increase your odds at generating a successful brand, but it will also make it easier for you to enjoy what you are doing. You will have far more fun catering to a niche that you are passionate about than a niche that you are only somewhat interested in being a part of, or that you are only a part of because it is known for being a profitable niche. For this reason, *only* pick a niche that you are passionate about and stick to that niche when it comes to online marketing.

You Must Improve Your Competency

The last part of setting yourself up for success in your brand is improving your competency. As a new online marketer, this will come in two layers for you, and you need to take both of these layers very seriously if you are going to generate ongoing success for your brand.

First, you need to recognize that you are in a position where you do not yet have a lot of knowledge or understanding of online marketing. Even if you have been studying it for some time, if you have not yet run a hands-on marketing business, you have not yet established the entire foundation of knowledge that you require in order to be fully successful with online marketing. Generating success with online marketing requires you to both have the knowledge of what it takes and the hands-on experience to get a feel for what it takes to be successful. If you want to approach your business in a way that will help you generate massive success, you need to be committed to laying a strong foundation of knowledge for yourself by finding out everything that you need to know to get started with online marketing. Reading this book is an excellent start, but you will want to continue building your foundational knowledge by applying what you have learned here and creating even more experience and knowledge for yourself and your success.

In addition to having foundational knowledge, you also need to keep yourself educated on what is going on in the online marketing world. Online marketing is constantly shifting, with new tools, techniques, and strategies regularly coming into play for people to take advantage of so that they can put their business in front of their clients in new and fun ways. If you want to achieve success in your industry and stay successful, you need to constantly improve your competency by updating your education around marketing. Keep yourself up to date on what is happening in the industry by educating yourself through new blogs, news articles, and books whenever possible. The more that you can educate yourself on marketing, online marketing, your industry, your niche audience, and your product, the better. Never grow complacent when it comes to this knowledge, as this knowledge is the basis for every decision that you make in your business. Without it, you find yourself struggling to create strong decisions that help you truly make a strong impact with your customers.

Chapter Summary

When it comes to running your online marketing business, you need to have a clear understanding that you are, in fact, running an online marketing business. A failure to take your business seriously can result in you creating a business that ultimately fails due to a lack of research, knowledge, or understanding of what needs to take place for you to succeed.

You need to be willing to look at every single part of your business professionally and make professional decisions for your business so that you are able to have the best success possible. You also need to be willing to put in the effort to research every aspect of your business and everything that could impact your business, and keep yourself up to date on this information. When it comes to running your online marketing business, knowledge is power, and you can gain it by staying educated on your industry, niche, audience, products or services, and general marketing and business-related information that could impact your business.

If you really want to be successful, you need to make sure that you start a business in a niche that you are passionate about. This way, you can build a brand that is personable and enjoyable to interact with, and that has a basic understanding of what customers need, and want, from a brand like yours. This is going to drastically improve the amount of credibility and trust that you gain from your customers, which directly impacts your income levels in your business.

Of course, in addition to passion, you also need a profitable market. The truth is: no matter how much knowledge you have or how great your product seems, if your market is not profitable, you are wasting your time. Remember: it is less foolish to quit on a market that clearly does not generate you any success than spending more money attempting to find a profitable audience within that market. Make sure that you are willing to call it quits if after 2-3 months you have still not generated any form of sales, because chances are you are marketing to an audience that is not buying. Use this perceived failure as a lesson to help you create a stronger brand and strategy going forward, and try again.

Chapter 8: The Winning Mindset

*"Whether you think you can
or you think you can't,
you're right."*
— Henry Ford

In addition to having the right perspective for approaching your online marketing business, you also need to have a winning mindset that will help you generate success with online marketing. Like with your perspective and approach, your mindset can play a massive role in whether or not you are actually going to succeed with your business.

The easiest way to understand why mindset is so important is to consider what it feels like to do something when you think you will succeed, versus what it feels like to do something when you think you are going to fail. According to psychologists, this basic mindset can actually play a huge impact on whether or not you are even set to succeed in the first place. A person who has a mindset that suggests that they will succeed no matter what it takes is a person who ultimately has the confidence and courage required to make it happen. The individual who believes that they can make a success is going to have far more resiliency and willingness to overcome adversity and continue working toward success, no matter what stands in their way. On the other hand, the person who does not believe that they will succeed often struggles to feel confident or capable enough of making anything happen. Quite often, they will quit before they even really go public with their business because they fear what might happen if they do not succeed. Alternatively, they do launch their business, but after their first major hardship, they quit and refuse to try again because they firmly believe that it is not possible for them to succeed.

In this chapter, we will discuss what you need to do to motivate yourself to succeed with your business. These mindset shifts are ones that you can implement to help you get into a "can do" frame of mind, while also helping you generate the mindset required to help you actually move through hardships and find the success that you are out to achieve.

Learn How to Motivate Yourself

Many people are entirely unaware of where motivation comes from, and so they have a hard time effectively motivating themselves to generate any level of motivation in themselves so that they have the energy and will to get things done. Entrepreneurs who are destined to succeed know how to motivate themselves for just about anything, no matter how mundane it might be so that they can guarantee their success. If you want to guarantee your success, you too are going to need to know how to motivate yourself so that you have the energy and drive to get things done, even when they are tasks that you are not particularly interested in doing. Since they all contribute to your success in the industry, it is worth it for you to put the effort in and learn about what it takes to motivate yourself and get the job done. The first thing to understand is that motivation truly does start in the mind. When you are motivated to do something, you mentally are prepared to exert the energy that it will take for you to mentally and physically get the job done. With this level of mental motivation, you can encourage yourself to push through anything that may lie in your way, as you will find a way to get through any challenges that you may face. Without the ability to mentally motivate yourself, no amount of energy physically, mentally, emotionally, or otherwise will help you get the job done.

When it comes to motivating yourself, each person is slightly different. You will have to find something that drives you to help you stay committed to seeing things through and creating success in your life. That being said, there are a few things that you can try to help you begin to motivate yourself. Through trying these things, you can cultivate a deeper sense of self-awareness that will help you ultimately determine what will continue to motivate you going forward.

The first thing that you can try when it comes to motivating yourself is understanding why you want to do said thing in the first place. What is that particular activity or task going to afford you in terms of something that you are working toward that you genuinely want? For example, with your online business, perhaps your motivating factor was that you wanted to replace your income with online marketing so that you could have more control over your time and income. In this case, every single time you need to get something done, you should remind yourself that it directly contributes to your ability to take control over your time and income, which directly serves something that you deeply desire.

Another way to motivate yourself is to make the task at hand seem less intimidating. At times, attempting to motivate yourself to complete a large task can be challenging because it feels like it will require too much time and energy to get it done. You might bargain with yourself by convincing yourself that you do not have enough time to finish it right now, so there is no point even getting started in the first place. Rather than letting your motivation falter due to the task seeming too large, chunk it down into smaller tasks and then motivate yourself to do each of the smaller tasks. Doing it this way can make the task feel much less intimidating and encourages you to motivate yourself to get the job done. Lastly, you can also make your activities more fun! Remember, you are the boss here, and you get to say what happens. If you are not having fun with the business that you are building, take the time to make it more fun so that you can enjoy yourself even more. The more you can have fun with the process, the more you will be able to motivate yourself because you actually enjoy doing the work you need to get done. Even the more mundane tasks can be made fun of by putting on some music, drinking your favorite beverage while you work, and rewarding yourself when the job is done. Over time, you will look forward to the experience, and these tasks won't seem so boring or difficult to develop motivation around.

Always Look for the Solution

Early on in the business, it can feel like there are many hurdles for you to overcome. With so much research and preparation to do, there are many steps that go into getting your business launched in the first place, which can make everything feel a lot more challenging. As well, because there are so many steps going into the process, there is much more that can go wrong, which can make it feel like a business is just one big challenge after another. The truth is: it does get easier once you get past the startup phase, so as long as you stay committed and continue to find a way through every challenge that you face, you are more likely to get to that point of everything becoming a lot easier.

When it comes to creating a strong mindset around these challenges, the best thing that you can do is have a solution-oriented mindset. A solution-oriented mindset is the type of mindset that allows you to look for solutions immediately upon recognizing that a challenge has been placed in front of you. Rather than grappling over how big the challenge might be and over what it will take for you to overcome it, thus psyching yourself out and making it feel even more challenging, you immediately start to look for solutions. Your primary goal is to find a way through the challenge, and so you begin to look for ways that you can do just that.

If a solution-oriented mindset does not come naturally to you, it is important that you begin to cultivate one. The stronger your solution-oriented mindset is, the more of an asset you will be to your business as you will always be focused on growth and going forward. You can begin to cultivate your solution-oriented mindset by conceptualizing theoretical problems that could arise in your business and identifying all of the possible solutions to those problems. The more that you practice searching for solutions, the easier it will be for you to find them when they truly are required.

Consistency Is Key in Your Success

When it comes to running a successful online business, consistency is crucial. Without consistency, you will struggle to create anything for yourself because you will always fall behind as soon as you get ahead. In business, consistency is not just about getting the job done; it is also about staying relevant and keeping a consistent and reliable brand in place for your clients.

For you, as the business owner, consistency means that you can feel confident that the job will always get done. Furthermore, it allows you to create a clear and manageable schedule that will allow you to consistently complete every task necessary for you to create your desired success in your business. When you are consistent, you know exactly what needs to be done when, and you know that each job is always done on time. As a result, your business runs smoothly and is always operating at its best to bring revenue in for you.

For your customers, consistency proves that you are a reliable brand and that they can trust you when it comes to purchasing products or services. When you are consistent, you prove that they are unlikely to have issues with receiving their products, receiving support around buying their products, and otherwise interacting with your brand. As a result, they know that they are likely to receive good service and that should anything go wrong, they can rely on you to help them.

In addition to you being reliable and trustworthy, consistency also keeps your brand relevant. When you are consistent, you continually put your brand in front of people so that they remember that you exist or so that they can find you in the first place. This way, you are regularly generating new traffic, and you are providing excellent service for the new traffic that you are attracting.

You can develop consistency easily by creating a simple schedule that you can follow with your business. There are many tools that you can enforce to help you improve your consistency, but schedules are the best ones. You can schedule out your content, the days that you are going to check on your analytics and design new marketing materials, the days that you order to develop new products or services for your business, and the days that you perform other industry-specific tasks for your business. By having everything organized and scheduled, you know exactly what needs to be done every single day, and you can feel confident that all of your tasks are being completed effectively.

Hone in on Your Courage to Jump

In business, your courage is one of your biggest assets as it gives you the strength that you need to take action, even when you are completely terrified of what is to come. Although some people seem to be born with ample courage to help them overcome anything, you do not need to have a strong, courageous streak to help you generate success in your business. You can certainly nurture your sense of confidence and courage so that you are more likely to jump in business, allowing you to take all of the right risks to success in your business.

One way that you can improve your confidence is through growing your knowledge around what it is that you are trying to achieve. Everyone is nervous when they are not entirely sure as to what it is they are doing, or what they need to be doing to generate success. With so much at stake, such as when it comes to running a business, it can be easy to understand why it feels so challenging to express courage in making decisions and taking risks. That being said, you can and should focus on increasing your sense of courage so that you can jump when you need to, and carry the confidence required to make every opportunity work in your favor.

One of the best ways to increase your courageousness and confidence is to start taking smaller risks regularly. As you do, you increase your risk tolerance and improve your confidence around doing things that feel uncomfortable or impossible. You also improve your ability to educate yourself on what risks are worth taking, and which are not, as you practice assessing the information you are given and making the best possible choices for you and your brand. As you continue to make these smaller risks, you can start making larger ones, too, and using the same skills that you have taught yourself with your smaller risks. This way, you can start to build up your confidence in larger risks as well.

In addition to building up your risk tolerance, another way to improve your courageousness is to choose to think positively. Be willing to keep an optimistic perspective on everything you do, and you will find that you are mentally prepared to take risks and opportunities that come your way. You can also reflect on the positive aspects of your risks each time you take them so that you can begin to see how courageous you already are and how courageous you can be when it comes to making the leap with things, such as your business.

Lastly, in the business, there is a huge "fake it 'til you make it" attitude around courageousness that actually seems to have a major impact on helping people succeed. With this perspective, people are given advice to act as if they are courageous and to behave like someone who has the confidence to back up what they are doing. This way, they are more likely to step outside of their comfort zone and take risks. Doing this frequently enough helps you increase your confidence while also developing skills that are beyond your present realm of abilities. As a result, you find yourself feeling far more confident in taking courageous risks to help grow your business.

Overcome Your Fear of Failure

Fear of failure is possibly the number one reason why most people never actually start their own online marketing business in the first place, particularly amongst those who wish to but are unwilling to pull the trigger to make it happen. When it comes to the idea of running your own business, it can be scary to consider the fact that there is a possibility that you could fail and that you could never actually produce any income from your business at all. This fear of failure is often about more than just failure itself, but about how you think about failure and what you think it means about who you are and what you have to offer the world.

Being afraid of starting your own business to the point where you are unwilling to even try could be due to the fact that you are afraid that other people will think that you are unworthy or bad at what you do. You might worry that you will be bullied, laughed at, or treated differently because you failed at launching a new business. You may even worry that you will believe these people and that you will start to see yourself as being less than or unworthy because of the failure that you may experience in your business. All of these can be scary to consider, and they can certainly make starting a new business challenging. However, they should not be enough to prevent you from even trying in the first place.

When it comes to this type of fear, the best thing you can do is reassure yourself that no matter what anyone thinks, you will never give in to the idea that you are not good enough because of some mistakes you have made. Develop a sense of confidence that no matter what happens, you will be proud of yourself for trying, and you are going to refuse to let anyone else change the way you feel about this. You are, in fact, brave for trying, and you are doing what many are too afraid to even try. This does not make you a failure or unworthy; this makes you brave and courageous, which are two honorable traits to have.

You can also shift your perspective by recognizing that some level of failure is inevitable and that virtually every successful business owner out there, no matter who they are, has experienced their fair share of failures along the way. Failure is not a surprise in business; it is almost a rite of passage that proves that you are, in fact, running a business. Using failure as a stepping stone to teach you how to move forward successfully is a powerful thing, and if anything, it will make others in the business world respect you even more.

So long as you can shift your own perspective around failure, you will feel a lot more confident in your ability to succeed in the online marketing business. Do not be afraid to sit with this one for a while and give yourself permission to fail, and permission to use that failure as a lesson to help you do better as you keep trying. You will be surprised at how much this simple talk with yourself can shift your attitude and help you grow your business.

Cultivate a Sense of Resiliency

Resiliency is a crucial mindset tool for anyone, but it is even more necessary when it comes to running your own business. The business world can be hard, and there are many challenges that you are going to face along the way that can make you question whether or not it is worth it for you to keep moving forward. These challenges or experiences can be burdensome and can make it feel like you have no chance of generating any form of success in your industry, so there is no point in moving forward. They are also absolutely necessary for you to move beyond if you are actually going to succeed.

Resiliency helps you continue to bounce back and keep moving, no matter how many times you are knocked down along the way. With resiliency, you are mentally prepared to overcome every setback, challenge, failure, and struggle that you face in your business with the type of gusto that is required for you to not only get past it but start thriving afterward.

As you cultivate a mindset fit for a business owner, you can develop your resiliency by talking to yourself in a way that improves your drive and willingness to succeed, no matter what it takes. By having an inner dialogue that says "I can do it" and "I can overcome anything," you build yourself up and develop the type of resiliency that helps you continue moving forward no matter what happens. You should also include phrases like "failure does not define me" and "I choose how I perceive each lesson in business" so that you are less likely to take everything personally. This way, when you do experience hardships, you are less likely to take them to heart and feel as though they are completely your fault. As a result, you are going to be far more effective at moving beyond your struggles and finding a way to succeed no matter what obstacle is set in front of you on your path to success.

Have Someone You Can Look Up To

Having someone to look up to is quite possibly one of the most powerful things that you can do for yourself when it comes to adopting the right mindset to help you succeed in business. When you have someone to look up to, you have someone who can inspire and motivate you to move forward no matter how challenging it may feel. You also have someone who encourages you to find new ways of doing things, and new opportunities to step outside of the box so that you can grow your business to be even more successful every single day.

When it comes to picking someone to look up to, ideally you should pick just one person. You can pick a role model if you have no one that you can look up to and work with directly, or you can pick a mentor who is going to help you by talking with you and encouraging you in business. Both a role model and a mentor will prove to be an asset to your business, no matter which you pick. You can also pick both if you feel that you have both someone you can look up to and someone that you work with. That being said, if you do work with a mentor, it should always be someone that you look up to so that you can feel confident that the advice and guidance you receive from them is going to help you run your business in a way that feels best for you.

After you have chosen who it is you are going to look up to, it is important that you regularly take the time to look up to them and check on how they are doing. Follow them, listen to what they are saying, and look to them for inspiration and guidance when you need to. Keep this person close in your inner circle, or at least in your newsfeed, so that you can regularly be inspired by them and motivated to keep going. The more that you keep this individual fresh in your mind, the more likely they will be able to influence you to do great things with your own business, which means that they will be serving their purpose, even if you never actually create a true friendship with them.

Chapter Summary

Your mindset is more of an asset to your business than nearly anything else that you could possibly possess or acquire in your business. If you want to be successful, you need to have the right mindset to help you do so as your mindset can make or break you. A person with a negative mindset will always be destined to believe that what they desire is impossible and that there is no way for them to generate any level of success in their lives. A person with a positive mindset will always believe that they can create what they desire and will seek to make it happen no matter what it takes.

Simply shifting to a more positive or optimistic mindset may not be enough for business, however. When it comes to business, you need to refine your mindset so that it works in your favor in every way possible when it comes to dealing with challenges in your business. You need to know how to motivate yourself, inspire yourself, and drive yourself to succeed so that you can always feel confident in your ability to get things done and grow your business. You also need to know how to look for solutions and remain consistent in your business so that you are always focused on achieving more growth. As well, you need to build your confidence and overcome your fears while developing your sense of resiliency. These three mindsets will help you massively when it comes to running your own business as they will provide you with the strength that you need to overcome and bounce back from any possible struggle that you may face in your business. Without this particular strength, you may feel too afraid to proceed after you have experienced any level of failure or setback along the way.

Chapter 9: It's Your Time

> *"This is a learning process,
> and sometimes you have to fall
> in order to learn things."*
> — Christine Korda

As you cultivate your business mindset and prepare yourself for success, I want to take a moment to champion you along the way. The fact that you are investing in understanding how businesses work and how you can run an online marketing business proves that you are fully capable of creating success with your chosen online marketing business, no matter what that may be. It takes a special, dedicated kind of person to choose to launch a business and then devote themselves to learning how to do so in the best possible way.

If you have had any doubts about your ability to succeed with online marketing, I encourage you to confront those doubts and recognize that you are more than capable of earning your desired income and time freedom through your online marketing business. Even if you are afraid of failure or worried that it may not go as planned, trust that your devotion to finding out how to make it work is strong enough to help you through any challenge that you may face. Although those challenges may be difficult, you have what it takes to be a success, and you are fully capable of doing just that.

Understand that as you launch your business, some of the challenges that you might face will exist beyond the business itself. Beyond challenges that you will have with finding the right niche with the right products and the right customers, you might also face challenges within yourself, or even within your social circle. Launching an online marketing business or any business for that matter can leave you feeling whether or not you are worthy or capable enough. You might find that you feel as though you are not good enough to make this work or that you are not lucky enough to be a success in your own business. This type of self-doubt regularly happens as the result of you, the individual launching the business, stepping outside of your comfort zone, and trying something new. At this point, you might feel like every doubtful or negative thing anyone has ever said to you or about you, or about online marketing, suddenly starts to feel incredibly true. You could question yourself in ways that you have never questioned yourself before, and it might start to feel like you are having a hard time remembering why you are worthy of the career that you are building for yourself, and the life that you are building for yourself.

This type of self-doubt and questioning is extremely normal and happens to virtually everyone who launches a business, so you are not alone in this experience. The best thing that you can do for yourself to help you overcome this self-doubt is to remember that every new experience has a learning curve, and running your own online business is no different. Although it might feel like it carries a much bigger sentiment and that any type of failure could be horrendous for you to face, this is not true. You are capable, you are confident, and you are worthy. You also can increase the point to which you believe in all of this so that you can feel even more capable, confident, and worthy of the success that you are creating for yourself. You can do so by regularly working on your mindset and increasing your willingness to believe in yourself and your ability to do great things for yourself.

The other type of pressure that you might face beyond the business itself is that which you get from the people around you. Many people have been wrongfully led to believe that online marketing is a scam and that there is no way that anyone could possibly be successful in online marketing. This, of course, is not true as many people are generating success in online marketing on a daily basis, which proves that it is certainly not a scam. The key is understanding that if you do not put in the effort, you are not going to see the results. Many people would rather blame the opportunity and call it a scam, rather than admit that they themselves were not educated or prepared enough to turn that opportunity into a success. Others still have never even looked into the opportunity for themselves, and instead, they simply hear from someone else that it is a scam and piggyback onto this belief.

The trouble with other people thinking your business is a scam is that you might always feel that you are defending yourself and explaining what you do to people so that they believe that you are actually capable of making money. Early on, before you are profitable, this can feel challenging because it might feel like you are constantly trying to get people to believe in you. This can lead to you feeling like you do not even believe in yourself, which could cause you to waiver in your optimism and your willingness to see your business through.

The best thing you can do about people who are not respectful about you and your endeavor is to cut them off from this part of your life or stop talking to them entirely, depending on who they are and how you know them. Not giving people access to this part of your life means that they do not have the opportunity to talk badly about your business, which completely prevents the uncomfortable feelings that come with being told that you are falling for a scam. As a result, you are less likely to foster their negative mindset around what you are doing, and you are more likely to stay motivated and continue working toward that success that you are more than ready to claim for yourself.

The only truth about your business, my friend, is that *it is time.*

I'm willing to bet that you have been considering this idea for quite some time now, but it has taken you awhile to take the leap. You may have been too afraid or uncertain to start educating yourself on the concept, for fear of not being able to make it work. But that's not true.

It's time for you to believe in yourself and trust that you have the strength, courage, and knowledge required to turn your dreams of running an online marketing business into a reality. It's time for you to take control over your income and your schedule and start doing business on your terms. It's time for you to achieve everything that you have attached to this dream, whether that includes you traveling the world, buying a beautiful home, or sending your kids to a great university — or all of the above.

It's time for you to pick what industry you want to run your business in and what type of business you want to run in the first place. It's time for you to decide how that business fits into your life and how it enriches your life in the best way possible. You are more than ready to let yourself do something that you are passionate about and earn an income doing it, and the world is ready for you to do so, too. Every single possible tool and piece of technology available for you to make this a success exists *right now,* and it is time for you to take advantage of it and put it to work so that you can achieve your dreams. *It's time for you to win.*

If you have reached this point and you are still totally clueless as to what you are actually going to do for your online business, then it's also time for you to decide on that! I have two excellent books written titled *Amazon FBA* and *Dropshipping for Beginners,* both of which are wonderful guides to help you get started with profitable online business models. Each of them also goes into incredible, step-by-step detail for how that particular business model works so that you can run your very own business online. I strongly encourage you to read them as a place to start if you have yet to figure out what you will do!

Above all else, you need to know and truly believe deep in your heart that you are *worthy* of having this. You are worthy of creating a business that helps you fulfill your wildest passions, and that feels like a dream come true in your life. You are deserving of creating the level of income that you desire to create and the level of freedom that you desire to have. You are worthy of allowing yourself the opportunity to try this new path out and enjoy it for every twist, turn, and challenge that it has to offer you. And you are more than capable of seeing this journey all the way through and achieving every goal you have set out for yourself along the way. All that's left for you to do is take the leap and make it official.

Say it with me: ***I'm the boss*!**

Conclusion

Running your own online marketing business is not just a fun idea; it's a smart one. In this modern world, knowing how to engage in online marketing and leverage it as a way to make money for yourself is an asset that virtually everyone can benefit from. With the current outlook of the economy and what lies ahead of us, online marketing may just be your best opportunity to cushion yourself against inflation and set yourself up for financial freedom no matter what happens. Beyond that, online marketing gives you the opportunity to be in business for yourself, which affords you many other benefits, including time freedom and the flexibility to work from anywhere that you like. This means that you no longer have to strap your career to a single location and hunker down for a wage that just doesn't seem worth it. With a successful online marketing business, you can completely liberate yourself from the current hustle and grind and rewrite your life and your entire future.

An opportunity that comes with so many massive benefits does not come without its own great number of challenges, however. When it comes to running your online marketing business, you need to be prepared for everything that might come your way. You need to recognize that this is a true business, and that means that the money is not exactly going to be easy in it. Although it becomes easier over time, it is not likely that you will be profitable right away. Furthermore, contrary to what certain media outlets might tell you, online marketing *requires you to have a startup budget, as you will* need to invest in all of the right tools and advertisements to get your business out there. That being said: online marketing can be incredibly rewarding, and it can lead to you having the opportunity to live the exact life that you desire to live without anyone being able to tell you otherwise.

I hope that through reading this book, you have developed a deeper sense of confidence in understanding what online marketing is, how it works, and what you need to be successful in this industry. By now, you should be feeling confident in the unique strategies that help you build sales funnels and drive traffic to your website so that you can earn more cash from your business. Remember, traffic is a crucial element of your business, so you should always be focused on how you can drive more traffic to your website. By leveraging both organic and paid advertising strategies, you can build a consistent and charismatic brand that also generates a massive amount of traffic for your website. The more that you can master the sales funnel process, the more sales you are going to make, and the more profitable you will become in your business.

As you go forward and start to develop your business, I encourage you to keep this book handy so that you can refer back to it along the way. It will be helpful for you to remember the important tools required for you to grow your business and how you can select the best possible tools for your business. When all else fails, always remember this basic rule of thumb: invest in the best possible service that you can afford with your current budget, and always seek out the services that you will be able to grow with going forward. You want to avoid having to move your services over to another provider at any point in the future, as the process can prove to be a massive headache.

As well, make sure that you keep your business as simplified as possible, especially early on. When you launch a new business, you already have so many different steps that need to be accomplished and perfected for you to be successful in your launch. You want to make sure that you are not adding any unnecessary steps as this can take your attention away from what is truly important, which can result in you having a poor foundation for your brand and business going forward. Always focus on putting your best attention and quality of work into every step of the process. You can always grow out your sales funnels and add more ways for people to come across your business in the future, so keep it as simple and straightforward as possible for now.

When you are ready to begin expanding out into new methods, make sure that you always grow one at a time. Take the time to perfect each new stream of incoming leads so that you can not only understand how it works but also turn it into a stream that generates conversions. This way, you are getting the maximum results from each new stream, which makes each one worthy of maintaining. Mastering one at a time will prove to be a valuable way of growth going forward, so do not waste your time being overzealous and take on too much at once.

In addition to putting all of this focus into your business itself, make sure that you also put this level of focus and energy into your mindset and your perspective. Remember, you are the biggest asset in your business, and your mindset is a massive part of that. Having the right mindset will make all of the difference in your ability to face and overcome challenges in your business, so it is worth your time and effort to invest in your mindset. Ideally, you should invest in your mindset every single day, both with your business and even outside of your business in your everyday life. You can never invest too much into yourself and your mindset!

Lastly, if you enjoyed this book and felt that it supported you in understanding online marketing and how to grow an online marketing business, I ask that you please review it on Amazon Kindle. Your honest feedback would be greatly appreciated.

Thank you.

George Brand.

www.ingramcontent.com/pod-product-compliance
Lightning Source LLC
Chambersburg PA
CBHW071406210526
45465CB00001B/277